THE QUESTION SETTLED.

A CAREFUL COMPARISON

OF

BIBLICAL AND MODERN SPIRITUALISM.

BY

MOSES HULL,

AUTHOR OF "THE CONTRAST," "WHICH," "LETTERS TO ELDER MILES GRANT," "BOTH SIDES," "THAT TERRIBLE QUESTION," "WOLF IN SHEEP'S CLOTHING," ETC., ETC.

"The thing that hath been, it is that which shall be; and that which is done is that which shall be done: and there is no new thing under the sun."

ECCLES. I. 9.

THIRD EDITION.

D. M. BENNETT:
LIBERAL AND SCIENTIFIC PUBLISHING HOUSE.
141 EIGHTH STREET, NEW YORK.

PREFACE.

A WISE man has said, "To the making of many books there is no end." This is literally true. Especially has spiritual literature increased so rapidly during the past few years, that it requires close attention to keep track of the matter almost daily issuing from its press. Yet, in our six years' effort in behalf of the doctrines advocated in these pages, we have again and again observed a niche that we had hoped ere this to have seen filled. Speaking of this a few weeks since, a friend suggested that it was our duty to stand in this gap. As we could see no signs of others who wield more instructive pens occupying this field, we have undertaken so to do. How well we have succeeded is to be decided by our readers.

When we contracted with our publishers, two months since, not a word of this volume was written: we, however, at that time supposed we had the plan of the work arranged; but our inspiration has stubbornly and persistently refused to follow our plan. The book has shaped itself, seemingly, almost without our aid.

When we took our pen, we seemed to see a huge chaotic mass of material to work into this book; and, until it was half done, we hoped to weave it all in: but, like the widow's oil, it has greatly multiplied; and, now that our book is done, we see so much more that has been left out of its pages than has been admitted, that we more strongly than ever see the necessity of another volume.

Should this volume meet the approbation of those for whom it was written, another may follow soon. This has been prepared amid the clash of spiritual arms. It has all been written and rewritten inside of eight weeks, while lecturing, preaching, debating, editing a journal, answering correspondents, &c. It has been written in the cars, in hotels, boarding-houses, dépôts, and sitting-rooms; in fact under the varying circumstances attendant upon the life of an itinerant.

Traveling as we have, we have had but little chance to examine libraries or consult books. Indeed, it was unnecessary, as our only aim has been to faithfully compare the Bible with modern phenomena and philosophy. If we have succeeded in this we are content.

MOSES HULL.

HOBART, IND., May, 1869.

CONTENTS.

CHAPTER I.

THE ADAPTATION OF SPIRITUALISM TO THE WANTS OF HUMANITY.

CHAPTER II.

THE MORAL TENDENCY OF SPIRITUALISM.

CHAPTER III.

BIBLE DOCTRINE OF ANGEL MINISTRY.

CHAPTER IV.

THE THREE PILLARS OF SPIRITUALISM.

CHAPTER V.

THE BIRTH OF THE SPIRIT.

CHAPTER VI.

ARE WE INFIDELS?

CHAPTER VII.

ARE WE DELUDED?

CHAPTER VIII.

OBJECTIONS ANSWERED.

THE QUESTION SETTLED.

CHAPTER I.

THE ADAPTATION OF SPIRITUALISM TO THE WANTS OF HUMANITY.

No Argument so good as that of Adaptation — Religions must adapt themselves to Men — Religions and Sciences have failed to demonstrate an After-Life — Two contradictory Chains of Thought in the Bible — Law forbidding Consultation with the Dead — Its Effect — Bible Writers in Doubt as to a Future — A Dialogue — Spiritualism convinces a Minister of his Immortality — Dying Minister in Despair — Why this Appetite for a Knowledge of a Future — Counterfeit Spiritualism an Evidence of a Genuine — Spiritualism not a Phantasm — Men love Spirit-Communion — Illustration — Spirits retain their Regard for Mortals — Is it Imagination — Where and What is the Land of the Dead — All interested in the Question — Sick Healed — Endless Progress — Theodore Parker — Abraham Lincoln — A Proof of the Truth of Spiritualism in its Beauty — Conclusion.

THERE is no argument so strong in favor of any hypothesis as that which shows unmistakably the adaptation of the theory to the work intended. A religious theory proving itself adapted to meet all the wants of the human soul comes with God's warrant in its hands. Having such *credentials* from the Almighty, but little else is needed to prove it true. As man is the highest type of the creation, yea, "the offspring of God" (see Acts xvii. 28), religions and theories must bend to man: he can not bend to them. They must come to him as he is, in a state of nature, and adapt themselves to his wants. The first inquiry which suggests itself is, What are the wants of the human soul? All answer, The first great want of the soul is an evidence of its own continued existence.

With all deference to other systems of religion and philosophy, Spiritualism is the only system which can make man know of his own immortality. Is man immortal? is a question which is now being propounded with more earnestness than ever before. How can the question be answered? If Science be consulted, she stands with drooping wings, looking down into the dark grave, and answers, "The knowledge is not with me. I am educated only in the past: I trace man from the primordial fires, through the granite rock, on through the mineral, vegetable, and animal kingdoms, to the grave: but I can see no farther." Science can not tell the strength of the disease now preying upon my body, nor yet the power of endurance my physical system may have; much less can it dive into the dark future, and grapple from its unwritten pages evidences of man's future condition. Poor blind Science! don't ask it to solve questions so entirely out of its reach. True, we may reason from the great law of design manifest everywhere, and from our reasonings draw the *hope* that this mundane existence will not wind up the course of man; but at best *it is only hope*. The soul demands *evidence* of its immortality. Where shall it be found?

If we recur to the Bible, we find two distinct and contradictory classes of ideas upon this subject running through that book. One chain of ideas comes from certain phenomena which were witnessed among the people; such as Samuel returning and holding a *tête-à-tête* with King Saul, Moses and Elias talking with Jesus on the mount, John's brother talking with him on the Island of Patmos, &c. See 1 Sam. xxviii. 14–20; Matt. xvii. 1–8; Rev. xxii. 8.

Though these facts are said to have occurred, they were in the most open violation of one of the strictest laws of the Jews, which reads as follows:—

"There shall not be found among you any one that maketh his son or his daughter to pass through the fire, or that useth divination, or a witch, or a charmer, or *a consulter of familiar spirits*, or a wizard, or *a necromancer*."—Deut. xviii. 10, 11.

Here is a law forbidding spirit-communion. It takes more courage than most people possess to enable them to violate such plain laws, with death as their penalty. The result, as might have been expected, was, that cases of spirit-communion were rare. Death they had before them constantly; graves they saw every day: but those who had passed on they did not see, did not dare to see them. The result was, many of them concluded they had no existence. Jacob, when he supposed his son Joseph to be dead, said, "Joseph is not" (Gen. xlii. 36). Rachel, being forbidden to consult her children, naturally enough concluded they were not (Jer. xxxi. 15). Isaiah says of the dead, "They are extinct; they are quenched as tow" (Is. xliii. 17). The writers of the Bible not only supposed, as a result of their being shut away from communication with the dead, that they had no existence, but they believed death to be a state of *eternal* nonentity. It was not Porphyry, Celsus, or "Julian the apostate," but Job, who said, "So he that goeth down to the grave shall come up no more" (Job vii. 9). David, the "man after God's own heart," did not leave it for Lord Bolingbroke or Pope to compose the poem which says, "Put not your trust in princes, nor in the son of man, in whom there is no help; for his breath goeth forth, he returneth to his earth: in that very day his thoughts perish" (Ps. cxlvi. 1–3). It was thirty centuries before the birth of the author of "The Age of Reason," that Solomon, the wise Jewish king, gave utterance to the following sentiment: —

"The living know that they shall die; but the dead know not any thing." — Eccl. ix. 5.

Not satisfied with uttering the atheistic sentiment of the unconsciousness of the dead, he proceeds to lock the doors of a future against them. Hear him: —

"*Neither have they any more a reward;* for the memory of them is forgotten. Also their love and their hatred is now perished; *neither have they any more a portion for ever in any thing that is done under the sun.*" — Eccl. ix. 5, 6.

All the above-mentioned passages express the most absolute infidelity concerning the future of man. These opinions can but be regarded as the legitimate result of the embargo put upon appealing to the dead for knowledge. Remove that restriction, let the Jew have the privilege which the heathen enjoyed, of consulting the dead, and how long could his infidelity have remained? Not long enough for Job to have said, —

"The grave is my house: I have made my bed in darkness. I have said to corruption, Thou art my father; to the worm, Thou art my mother and my sister. And where is now my hope? As for my hope, who shall see it? They shall go down to the bars of the pit when our rest together is in the dust." — Job xvii. 13–16.

If the Bible writers themselves, for whom a plenary inspiration is claimed, who, it is supposed, enjoyed all the evidences of immortality, were so unbelieving concerning the future, is it any wonder that the world today has so nearly run into atheism on that subject? If the position assumed be correct, that the elements of the infidelity of the Jews had an origin in their non-intercourse with the dead; that, in proportion as that people transcended their legal rights, and held occasional converse with visitants from the other side, their unbelief was supplanted by knowledge, — then we may safely affirm, that, without Spiritualism, there *is* no positive evidence of a future life.

When traveling on a certain occasion through Canada, the writer was introduced to a Baptist minister. As the prefix "Reverend" was used in his introduction, the gentleman of course supposed him to be an evangelical minister. Being curious to know whether this minister could find any evidence of another world, independent of Spiritualism, he commenced a conversation which resulted in the following dialogue: —

Hull. — How is the cause of religion in Canada?

Minister. — All is well. We had glorious revivals through these parts last winter. Of course, matters have cooled down somewhat; yet, with many, the work seems to be deep and lasting. How, may I ask, is the good cause in Michigan?

H. — We are having trouble there. There are a great many thinkers in that State, and among them a large proportion of materialists who deny immortality; and we find them hard to meet.

M. — Ah! I see no trouble in meeting them, especially if they believe the Bible. Why don't you tell them that Samuel returned to talk with Saul? This he never could have done had not he been immortal.

H. — True enough. That could be used, for aught I know, in Canada; but it does not do to use it in Michigan. There are in that State about twenty-five thousand Spiritualists; and, were you to quote that text, every one of them would claim you as being on their side of the question; for, if the text proves any thing, it proves Samuel was immortal by the fact of his having returned and communicated. We do not wish, when battling with atheists and materialists, to put a club into the hands of the Spiritualists with which to beat our brains out when we undertake to deny Spiritualism.

M. — True; but could you not tell them of the appearance of Moses and Elias on the Mount of Transfiguration?

H. — Yes; but that, too, if it proves any thing, proves the continued life of the parties by their returning.

M. — Yes, yes; but should we reject a truth because the Spiritualists believe it?

H. — Certainly not. But is there no way to prove immortality, without resorting to texts, which, if they prove any thing, prove Spiritualism?

M. — The fact is, my belief in immortality does not hang upon biblical expressions. *I know man is immortal.*

H. — You are the man I want to see. Tell me how you know it.

M. — Last Saturday I was called to the bedside of a dying sister: while we were watching for the last breath, she suddenly brightened up, and said, "See there! do you see?" — "See what?" I said. "There is my sister, and one who I guess is Jesus: they have come for me." Saying this, she expired. Now I can not think this all deception. God is too good to let one who had trusted him all the days of her life die so deceived.

H. — So I think; but *that* is Spiritualism. And now let me confess that I am a Spiritualist. I have talked thus with you to see if you had any evidence of immortality which would not prove Spiritualism.

M. — I do not see that we are bound to reject a truth because Spiritualists believe it.

This last sentence, though true, does not present the matter fairly. Every system of religion in the land lives and is sustained by its spiritual element. The question was not, "Shall I reject the evidence of immortality presented to my dying sister?" but, "Is there any evidence, except that which comes in such a way, that, if it proves any thing, it proves Spiritualism?"

The world demands to-day, above all things, the evidence of immortality. All demand it. As the mother takes the last look at the cold, dead body of her son, and imprints a kiss on his colorless cheek, she involuntarily exclaims, "*Shall I see my child again?*" Then let the minister point her to some biblical declaration, and her very soul will revolt at it; and she will inwardly, if not outwardly, exclaim, "Such authoritative *ipse dixits* may do under ordinary circumstances; but they fail to reach a mother's heart in an extremity like this." What will convince that mother? "Is there no balm in Gilead? is there no physician there?" She naturally feels, "If my son lives, why does he not take this burden from my heart? Has he lost all interest in me? Oh for one breeze from the summer-land (if there be such a country), just one rap, one test, one evidence, that my son still lives and thinks!"

Now the Spiritualist believes that that boy *can* come back and communicate with his mother; that he *can* say, "Mother, I am alive!" Reader, don't you *wish* it was true? Wouldn't you *make* it true if you had the making of the truth? If these questions were asked of the great body of humanity, would *one single voice* be found to say, "No"?

Once upon a time, we were invited to the bedside of a dying minister, whom we had long known to be a *good* man and a consistent Christian, if there ever was one: to say the least, his daily life was a better epistle than Paul ever wrote. The minister was taken suddenly with hemorrhage of the lungs, and drew rapidly near the gates of physical dissolution. Looking up to us, he faltered out, "Brother Hull, do *you* believe in the *resurrection* of the *dead?*"

"Why," said we, "you have heard us preach on that question many times: did you think we would preach what we did not believe?" He responded, "I was taught to believe it; but I know now, for the first time, that I never did. I received it from my teachers and my Bible without investigating. I am now dying; and I frankly acknowledge that I do not believe this body can again be gathered. I can not see that there is a future for man." After reasoning with the man nearly an hour, we ventured to ask, "Are you now satisfied?" He responded, "I am dying now: I can not talk. My request is for you to preach my funeral-discourse; and don't let one who hears it, die, as I am dying now, without any hope of a beyond."

Under the influence of this scene, we could but exclaim, "If there is *not* another world, what a pity there is not! and, if there *is*, what a pity that God did not give us a better knowledge of it!" Without *Spiritualism* there *is* no evidence of another world.

Now we would inquire, Is this appetite for a *beyond* the only one God has left ungratified? or, having granted us this boon, has he left us without any possibility of knowing that there is life when the earthly life has ceased, until by experience we know of the better country? It can not be that God, who has done all in his power for man, has left us thus to grope in darkness. No: when every other source of evidence has been set aside as unsatisfactory, Spiritualism comes to our relief; thus proving itself, in this respect at least, adapted to the needs of humanity.

Evidences of another life, given through Spiritualism, are many of them of such a character, that those who have witnessed them find no room for doubts. That there are cases of deception, that there are lying mountebanks who wear the fair garments of Spiritualism as a cloak for their iniquity, does not affect the genuine manifestations more than a genuine bank-bill would be affected by counterfeits issued on its credit. Nay, do not counterfeits prove the existence of a true coin, which is worthy of counterfeiting? Men do not counterfeit copper coin: it is too cheap. How strangely beside themselves men get when they conclude there is no genuine Spiritualism because they have found a counterfeit! Profound logic that! When such men as Robert Owen, Robert Hare, Robert Dale Owen, and hundreds of others whom we might mention, who have all their lives, up to the time of their communion with the departed, doubted whether there was another life, are, through Spiritualism, so perfectly convinced of it, that no room is left for a doubt, and they are ever after not only believers, but open advocates of immortality, we are led to ask, Is any other argument needed to show that Spiritualism is perfectly adapted to meet that earnest longing of the human heart for a knowledge of endless life?

Now, we ask, Is not immortality a natural want? and, if man is immortal, is not the evidence of the fact a want natural to him? Spiritualism is found equal to the task of supplying that need. Has it not in this proved itself adapted to the wants of man? No other religion has done so much.

Is it objected that the evidence is not real? that only the *gullible* are deceived by it? Admit it, and what is the result? Man is a poor worm, either without immortality, or, if immortal, without any evidence of the fact. All hope pertaining to the future is idle. All our prospects are blasted. Religion is a solomn *farce*, and man of all creatures the most miserable, placed on the earth, given a taste of life, made to enjoy immortality, and yet his highest joys and brightest anticipations all imagination. And is it so? Has not the Giver of all good been able to make the reality as glorious as man, without any image before him, could paint the ideal? Tell us that day does not follow night, that water does not quench thirst, that it is only fanatics who imagine that the sun shines, that this life is a miserable *phantasm;* but do not tell us that the seeds of happiness sown in the human soul by this beautiful belief will never grow.

Even admitting that man could know of another world without Spiritualism, yet who would not hold sweet communion with those on the other side? We are all social beings. We love social converse; nor is that love confined to the living. The true wife does not cease to love her husband as soon as he passes from her sight: that husband, whose voice was once sweet to her, and whose friendly counsel was her greatest solace, still lives. Is it not natural that the wife should long for communion with the one whose life was almost a part of her being?

To illustrate: a mother had two sons, James and John, whom she loved as her own life; but when traitors fired into our flag, and trampled it under foot, she gave them up to defend their country. In the course of the battle, James was killed; but John, after passing through severe engagements, returns home a triumphant conqueror. How the loving mother hails her son! With what eagerness does she grasp his hardened hand! With what outgushing of soul does she imprint her kisses upon his sun-browned cheek! How proudly she watches his every move! With what heartfelt joy does she welcome him to the place at the table made vacant by his absence! And as he relates his experiences on the battle-fields, in forced marches, in prison-pens, how her very soul drinks his every word! Now, who can think that she forgets James, who, fired with the same patriotism, went, but never returned? How would her soul rejoice, could James come back from the other side, and fill *his* vacant chair, and relate the experiences *he* has had since his birth into the better world! Is there one on earth who has a friend in spirit-life, but that would like to see and converse with that friend? The spiritual philosophy says, Such communion awaits you. Who does not wish it correct on that point? Then it is adapted to meet the wants of man.

Not only is spirit-communion desirable for lonely ones yet clothed in mortality, but departed spirits themselves must long for the privilege of loving and blessing dear ones whom they have left behind.

Were the angel of death to summon us this moment to the better land, we should leave a wife and four daughters, whom we love as we love our own soul. They may not be very much in the world; but they are all the world to us. We remember that this world is sometimes cold and heartless, especially toward the feminine half of humanity. Woman is not legally, socially, and politically man's equal; often compelled to work for less than half wages, and sometimes driven to the alternative of stealing or starving, or, even worse than either, compelled to sell her virtue for the bread and butter the world owes her. Could we think of going to heaven and singing praises, and our wife and daughters driven to such lives as these, — we not even having the privilege of looking over its battlements, and asking, How fares thy soul? Nay; rather put us into an orthodox hell, with the privilege of an occasional respite to bless those left behind, than thus to shut us away from those who need a husband's love and a father's counsel. If this communion be not true, we chide with Almighty God. Has he made that false which man needs, and that true which is so illy adapted to meet his wants? Has the Devil beaten God so badly, and got the best and *prettiest* theory after all? Believe it who can: we can not. Nay! the father, mother, brother, or sister who crossed the stream of death before us, *can not* lose their interest in those left behind.

Another reason why the soul longs for Spiritualism is, that each and every one is personally interested in knowing what there is in reserve for him. The realities of another world, if there be another, we must soon taste. How shall we find things over there? is a query which can not be expelled from any mind. How natural the query! Were we emigrating to some distant country, how anxiously would we try to learn something of its location, climate, soil, timber, inhabitants, &c.! and how should we find out? In no other way than by consulting those who have been there. The truth is, we are all emigrants — to what place? If to a haven "from whose bourn no traveler returns," how dark the prospect ahead! No wonder that Job said, "A land of darkness as darkness itself." Certain it is we can learn nothing of that world, only as we learn it from those who have been there. Then how beautiful the thought, that those on the other shore can draw the curtain aside, as did Samuel of old, and give us news concerning their whereabouts and condition!

In hours of weary sadness, when cares are pressing heavily upon us, and we weary even of life itself, how sweet to have such spirits as Miss A. W. Sprague come through such mediums as Miss Lizzie Doten; and after announcing that—

"I come, I come, from my spirit-home,
Like a bird in the early spring,
To the loved ones here, whom my heart holds dear,
A message of love to bring,"

and telling us that—

"The heavens are wide, but they can not divide
The spirits whom love makes free!
The green old earth, and the land of my birth,
With its homes, are still dear to me,"

to go on and give such glowing descriptions of the heavenly country, that, while reading, we sometimes quite forget that we belong to earth!

"We'll be there, we'll be there, in a little while,
We'll join the pure and the blest,
We'll have the palm, the robe, the crown,
And for ever be at rest."

Oh, glorious thought! How our soul fills with rapture as we contemplate the summer-land as described by those who have tasted its fruit, breathed its air, traversed its fields, and bathed in its exhilarating waters!

Spiritualism professes to heal the sick. There are persons (mediums) who profess, under favorable conditions, to come so *en rapport* with the spirit-world as to enter into certain magnetic relations with it, by which, by a touch, they can heal disease. Thus the blind have been made to see, the deaf to hear, and even the insane have, by this power, been restored to sanity. Call this all imagination! How glorious such an imagination! Why can it not be true? Would not a religion which would do what some imagine Spiritualism is doing, just meet the wants of the world? What a pity that such a religion should lack only the element of truth!

One more point: the idea of endless progression, as taught in Spiritualism, is certainly one of the most beautiful thoughts that ever entered the human brain. If that be true, not only are such men as Newton, Locke, Bacon, Washington, Jefferson, Clay, Webster, Douglas, and Lincoln alive to-day; but they live for a purpose. They are interested in matters of theology and jurisprudence as much to-day as when they wore their own bodies. Let two cases illustrate our ideas; and who shall they be? One we will select from the theological, and one from the political world. From the religious world, we could not make a better selection than Theodore Parker. From the political world, Abraham Lincoln will be the man of our choice.

It is unnecessary for us to say a word in Mr. Parker's praise. Most of our readers know with what steady purpose his noble heart was devoted to every reform. Sinners feared him more than all the other ministers of New England put together. He always asked, not, What will bring the praise, honor, or wealth of the world? but, What is right? In the winter of

1857–'58, the people of New England were insane with religious excitement, and yet, in their revival meetings, would publicly rebuke one who dared to remember the poor slave in his chains. Mr. Parker occupied Music Hall in Boston, and, from Sunday to Sunday, preached to the people of "The Revival of Religion which we *need*," — a revival which breaks every yoke, and tears away every burden; which pays the milliner and dress-maker in proportion as it does the lawyer, doctor, or minister; which would occasionally let a poor servant-girl make a summer tour to Europe, and let her pay go on the same as though she were a minister: in fact, a revival which sanctifies the *kitchen* as well as the *pulpit.* Such preaching was too much for New-England Puritanism; and the result was, the "baptized" and "sanctified" infidels to the purer religion held prayer-meetings to pray him out of the world. And when the news came from the "sunny South" that Theodore Parker was dead, what rejoicing and thanksgiving! "One infidel out of the world!" "We'll hear no more of Theodore Parker. He is dead and gone!" How mistaken!

Theodore Parker is not dead. He is here now. His voice rings as melodiously, truthfully, and harmoniously in behalf of every reform as when he spoke through his own organism. The cause of humanity, which is the cause of God, lies as near his heart as ever. Still he follows the waymarks of those ahead of him, and beckons those behind to follow on. He, with all of us, can spend an eternity in exploring the vast oceans of knowledge. As here, he lives to learn; and after the longest imaginable period, after he has traversed field after field that he does not now know exists, he will see so much more ahead of him than there is in the past, that he can but use the sentiment of Sir Isaac Newton: "I seem to myself like a little child, picking up pebbles on the shore, while the whole ocean lies unexplored before me."

Now, as to the case of Abraham Lincoln, the lamented martyr, — where is he? He, too, gave his life for the cause of humanity, — gave liberty to more slaves than any other one man in the world. Again we ask, Where is "Honest Abe"? This noble patriot happened not to be fortunate enough to belong to a church. He died out of Christ. The church called him an infidel. He died in a theater, with nothing to recommend him but his intelligence, his patriotism, and his unswerving honest fidelity. Again we ask, Where is he? Church systems can not save him. Do we press the question too close? We will change it, and ask, Where is "Stonewall Jackson" the traitor, the baptized evangelical minister! — one who never went into the battle-field to spill the pure, innocent blood of the North without first getting down upon his knees, and asking God to help him with blood to tighten the chains of slavery on four millions of innocent human beings? He was a Christian after the "straitest sect." Of course, he is in heaven, singing songs, and feasting his righteous eyes upon the sight of Abraham Lincoln in hell. Reader, do you think the groans and shrieks of Mr. Lincoln in the "fiery pit" are music in the pious ears of Stonewall Jackson?

Do you say you do not believe that Mr. Lincoln is in hell? Then where is he? If he is in heaven, away goes the orthodox scheme of salvation. Men are outgrowing and getting better than their religions, and are not willing to let good men out of the church go where their systems assign them. Look from another standpoint. Is Mr. Lincoln in heaven? What is he doing there? Sitting down and singing songs,

> "Where congregations ne'er break up,
> And sabbaths never end"?

No. Tell us that Mr. Lincoln is telling stories, and we may incline to believe it; but song-singing or flattering the approbativeness of Jehovah is not his business. Then what is he doing? Let Spiritualism answer.

He bade farewell to earthly friends to join the host of immortal statesmen, to assist on the other side in carrying out the work so nobly commenced in this life. At present writing, we seem to be carried back to his birth into spirit-life, and see him clasped in the arms of such men as George Washington. Next he is welcomed to the land where all anxiety is gone, by such patriots as Adams, Monroe, Hancock, Jefferson, Clay, Webster, and Douglas; all bidding him join the host of immortal statesmen, and work in their congress, where his labors will be crowned with tenfold the success which attended his efforts here. Is that all? No. Old John Brown, who went before Lincoln, as John the Baptist went before Jesus, whose soul had been marching on for six years, next extends his hand, and welcomes Lincoln as slavery's last martyr. Look again, and see the tens of thousands of "brave boys," whose blood has stained and fattened the fair fields of the South, give him the right hand of fellowship, and welcome him to their celestial army. But a more affecting sight yet awaits us. The poor slave, whose bitter experience tells more effectually than all things else the horrors and degradation of slavery, approaches the emancipator, the last to drink the bitter cup of martyrdom in consequence of the institution; and, as he throws his black arms around his neck, we seem to hear him cry out, "*Bress de Lord!*" whereupon myriads freed by his Emancipation Proclamation join in bidding him welcome to that land where the servant is free from his master.

Such, dear reader, is Spiritualism. Now, we ask, can a theory be so beautiful, so well adapted to man, and not be true? Has the God of truth been so badly beaten, that man's imagination has painted visions which so far excel the reality? Don't tell it! An omnipotent God who does all he can for man can make the reality more than man, in the highest flight of his imaginings, can paint the future. Have no fear of overdrawing in painting the beauty and reality of the "better country." It can not be done. There is another world, — one of which the present is only a reflection. There joy is great and lasting.

> "Its glorious light is the smile of God;
>   Its brooding atmosphere holy peace;
> The breath of its life is the spirit of love;
>   And earth's warring passions and longings cease.
> Touch us, O death, with thy mystic wand,
> And bring us into the summer-land."

CHAPTER II.

THE MORAL TENDENCY OF SPIRITUALISM.

A Natural Query — Jesus regarded as a Blasphemer and a Devil — Every new System passes an Era of Calumny — Persecution purifies — What Good has Spiritualism done — Opponents unfair — Immorality in the Churches — Religious Systems not responsible for Errors of their Adherents — None perfect — All are God-makers — Men worship their own Opinions — Shortcomings of Bible Saints — Jewish Church — Testimony of Jeremiah — Of Jesus — Of Paul — Drunkenness and "Free-lovism" in the Early Church — Errors of Noah — Abraham — Isaac — Jacob — The twelve Patriarchs — Moses — Joshua — Samuel — David — Solomon — Jesus — Peter — Paul — Spiritualism a Reform School — Welcomes Sinners — Churches disfellowship Sinners — Illustrative Case — "Come and go with us" — Phenomenal Spiritualism — It appeals to our deepest social Feelings — The Theory of Spiritualism the best moral Governor — Its Philosophy — A Contrast — Orthodoxy and Heathenism — Eternal Punishment for Sin — Familiar Story — Is it Just — Living and Dying in Heaven — No Barriers to Sin — No moral Change at Death — Illustration — We are Authors of our Destinies — Conclusion.

WHEN a new theological or philosophical aspirant to public favor forces itself upon the people, the query very naturally arises, What is its moral character? This is as it should be. A theory which is morally evil can not be theologically or philosophically good. Still, may we not, in challenging the virtues of new systems, often look at them through glasses colored by old, dilapidated theories, and hence see vice where only virtue exists? It was so anciently. When Jesus presented his claims, the response was, "This man is not of God, because he keepeth not the sabbath-day" (John ix. 16).

Thus, judging by the old Jewish standard, the Nazarene was deserving of nothing better than death. Yet his system has lived long enough to gain a reputation; he has come to be considered more pure than his accusers, who were in such great fear, lest he, by his example or precepts, should corrupt the morals of society. He who was once regarded as a devil (Matt. xii. 24) is now worshiped as a God; thus,

> "The demons of our sires
> Become the saints that we adore."

No churchman found it any trouble in the days of Jesus and Paul to prove them guilty of blasphemy. See John ix. 33; Matt. xxvi. 65; Acts xiii. 44–50. So, now, churchmen may see huge "camels" of immorality in the Spiritualism of to-day, when only "gnats" exist. While it is but just to investigate the morals of any new system of religion, the insinuations which popular opinion has thrown out after every system while in its infancy are unjust. Yet the systems thus misrepresented will not by that means sustain a permanent injury. Some will, for the time being, be deterred from investigating; but that will only be transitory. The time will come when the falsehoods of opposers will appear; then men will flock to the standard of the slandered theory with more than double the zeal that otherwise would have characterized them in its support.

Spiritualism, like all other new truths, has been so unfortunate, or fortunate, rather, as to be compelled to pass through the ordeal of calumny and slander. Like gold, purified in the fire, it will emerge from out the grasp of its persecutors and slanderers, purified, "made white, and tried."

Let an advocate of the spiritual philosophy go to a place where the people know nothing of its teachings, and how soon his preaching is met with the question, What good has Spiritualism done in the world? Some even lack the modesty to present their objection in the form of a question: they usually commence their opposition by roundly asserting that Spiritualism never has done any good in the world; that it is evil, and "*only* evil continually;" its aim is to overthrow every good institution, and people the infernal regions with millions who otherwise would have entered the world of "celestial glory." Thus every possible effort is made to get the idea "grounded and settled" in the hearts of the people, that there is something in Spiritualism calculated to destroy the morals of its adherents. Cases of immorality among Spiritualists are magnified, and presented to the world as evidence of the downward tendency of Spiritualism.

This mode of argumentation is unfair. The question is not, Are there immoral Spiritualists? but, Does Spiritualism lead men and women who otherwise would be chaste and virtuous to lives of degradation? We claim that it does not; that its tendency is in the other direction. We are willing to pledge ourself to find more cases of immorality in any of the evangelical churches than any person can find among the Spiritualists of America. What shall be done when cases of immorality are found in the churches? Shall they be held up as evidences of the immoral tendency of Christianity? or shall we say, as do others, that "it is human to err," and look upon their errors as mistakes and shortcomings of humanity, rather than evidence of the damnable tendency of their religion?

If the errors of Christian people are only evidences of the frailty of humanity, may not the errors of Spiritualists be attributed to the same source? The truth is, "there is none good, no, not one." All are imperfect. Men differ only in *degree;* none walk by an infallible standard: yet some come nearer the standard erected by the world than others. No one is absolutely good, even in his own estimation. Not one upon earth but that is "found wanting," even when weighed in scales of his own making. No one ever yet worshiped a God that he did not make himself. "Man makes God in his own image" is a decided improvement on biblical phraseology. Another proverb might be improved by having it read, "An honest God is the noblest work of man."

The truth is, the Infinite never was fully comprehended by the finite; but all have their ideas of Deity. These ideas we worship, and call God; and as the ideas of one have fallen below or reached beyond those of another, so one has worshiped a more pure or impure god, as the case might be, than another. In theology, men have been wont to embody all that they can imagine that is pure, good, true, and lovely, and call that God, and worship it as such. As we strive in our every-day life to imitate the character of the god we worship, we approach, by constant practice, nearer to it yet we are only following on; we can only advance in proportion as our ideal god advances: hence our theory must eternally be ahead of our practice. So, judging every man by his own theory, he is not exactly correct in his life. The only query then is, Who are nearest the true standard, — Spiritualists or others?

Were the religion of any denomination to be judged by the shortcomings of its members, what church could stand? This mode of judging of any religious theory is illogical and unfair; yet it is that adopted by the opponents of Spiritualism. Try even the religion of Bible times — that of the prophets and apostles themselves — by this standard, and upon its banners will be inscribed, "Mene, Mene, Tekel."

As it is no part of our business to hunt out the shortcomings of any sect or party, a few illustrations must suffice. A paragraph or two will sufficiently illustrate the shortcomings of Bible people, living in Bible times. To whom shall we go for evidence? Shall we consult Porphyry, Celsus, Julian the apostate, or more modern infidels? Shall Hume, Voltaire, or Paine testify? No. Let us go to Bible-makers themselves.

Jeremiah, an ancient medium, a preacher of the Jewish religion, in addressing God's ancient people, said, —

"Behold, ye trust in lying words, that can not profit. Will ye steal, murder, and swear falsely, and burn incense unto Baal, and walk after other gods whom ye know not, and come and stand before me in this house, which is called by my name, and say, We are delivered to do these abominations? Is this house, which is called by my name, become a den of robbers in your eyes? Behold! even I have seen it, saith the Lord." — Jer. vii. 8–11.

Is it so? Were God's ancient people, who enjoyed the labors of the inspired prophets, such characters?

Liars, thieves, murderers, and perjured persons constitute the church of God in the days of Jeremiah! And is this the fountain whence Christianity springs? Good heavens! Let us hear no more of immoral Spiritualists. Allowing that Jeremiah tells the truth, is it any wonder that Jesus said, "It is written that my house shall be a house of prayer; but you have made it a den of thieves"? — Matt. xxi. 13.

Hundreds of quotations from the Bible might be given, showing that these lamentations are not freaks of the imagination of Jeremiah and Jesus, but *real truths.* As the object of this chapter is not to prove that other religions have not made good men, but that Spiritualism has not made bad men, we will, with one more quotation from the Old Testament, close its evidence upon this subject. Hosea, another of Israel's ancient teachers, said of the church of his day, "By swearing and lying and killing and stealing and committing adultery, they break out, and blood toucheth blood."— Hos. iv. 2.

Such extracts from Bible writers need no comment. The religion of the Jews failed to reform them: its tendency may have been good, but was not strong enough to hold a rebellious people. Now, shall we take the shortcomings of the Jewish people as evidence of the immoral tendency of their religion? Such is the course pursued by anti-Spiritualists in regard to the errors and shortcomings of those who believe that heaven and earth are in communion.

Even Christianity, anciently as well as in modern times, failed to reform those who embraced it. The church at Corinth was composed of such a notorious set of drunkards, that it was unwise and unsafe to administer to them the emblems of the broken body and spilled blood of Jesus, one of their gods: the first one that got the wine got drunk on it, and others were compelled to go away without any, doubtless not so much regretting their failure to celebrate their Lord's death, as the fact that they were not the lucky one who got the first pull at the wine. Hear Paul plainly state the facts: —

"Now this I declare to you: I praise you not, that ye come together not for better, but for worse. For first of all, when you come together in the church, I hear that there be divisions among you; and I partly believe it. For in eating, every one of you taketh before other his own supper, and one is hungry, and another is drunken." — 1 Cor. xi. 17–21.

Is it true that the ancient church — those who enjoyed the immediate labors of the apostles — could not come together for a religious meeting without quarreling, and finally having their meetings terminate in a drunken row? Shall we say that Christianity led to their drunken quarrels? No. It only failed to prevent them. So Spiritualism may, in some instances, for a time, fail to accomplish the great work designed to be brought about by it; yet those who accuse it of having an immoral tendency accuse it wrongfully.

The chief charge brought against Spiritualism is that of "free love." By this, opponents mean a promiscuous intermingling of the sexes, opposed alike to the laws of God and man. While we distinctly deny that Spiritualism has any tendency to make man or woman untrue in any sense whatever, we answer, Suppose Spiritualism does tend in that direction; suppose Spiritualism leads to licentiousness, and that in the worst form that the meanest opponent of Spiritualism can imagine, — is it any worse than that which has ever obtained among the churches ? Who can find a case that will compare in vileness with that stated by Paul ? Hear him : —

" It is reported commonly that there is fornication among you, *and such fornication as is not so much as mentioned among the Gentiles, that a man should have his father's wife.*" — 1 Cor. v. 1.

This case is not among the Gentiles, Heathens, Spiritualists, or any other class of sinners, but in the church, under the immediate labors of the apostles. How did the ancient church like such things ? Did its members regret that they had such characters in its fold ? Not a bit of it : they were proud of it. Paul says, —

" And ye are puffed up, and have not rather mourned that he that hath done this deed might be taken away from among you." — 1 Cor. v. 2.

While the church in its very foundation, under the direct labors of its founders, is proud to acknowledge such lewdness, let its children of the nineteenth century examine the block whence they were hewn, and consider whether they were not " born of fornication," before accusing others at too great a rate.

A few words on the errors of Spiritualists, if thrown out in the right spirit, may help them to be better men and women. But how would a chapter look devoted to the errors of Bible saints ? For instance, parade the following, as a few specimens of the errors of those through whom God anciently manifested himself : —

Noah got drunk, cursed his grandson, and, some think, brought slavery upon a whole race, though guilty of no crime. — Gen. ix. 21–25.

Just and righteous Lot (2 Pet. ii. 20-25) became beastly intoxicated, and committed incest with his two daughters, each of whom had a child by her own father. — Gen. xix. 31–38.

Abraham had a plurality of wives and concubines, abandoned his own son, and left him to die in the wilderness, married his own sister, denied his own wife, and attempted to kill his only legitimate son. — Gen. xii. 13, 19; xiv. 2–4; xv. 2–5, 12; xxi. 10–14; xxii. 1–11.

Isaac followed in the path of his father, and denied his wife. — Gen. xxvi. 6.

Jacob took advantage of his brother's starving condition, and cheated him out of his birthright, by lying to and deceiving his old blind father, and thus succeeded in stealing his brother's blessing; had two wives and several concubines; stole his father-in-law's cattle, &c. — Gen. xxv. 32, 33; xxvii. 19; xxix. 18–30; xxx. 5; verse 40.

His twelve sons followed the example of their father, insomuch that there is hardly a crime in the catalogue of which they were not guilty.

Moses' first public act was to commit a murder. He advises his brethren to steal, or borrow and run away with the borrowed goods, which is the same thing; orders the destruction of innocent babes, and the captivating of females for the purpose of prostituting them to the gratification of the base lusts of the Jewish soldiery. — Exod. ii. 12; Num. xxxi. 17, 18.

Joshua was perhaps the greatest butcher of men and women that ever lived. The sun is even represented as obeying his command to stand still while he commits wholesale murder. — Josh. x. 13.

Samuel hewed an old, innocent, helpless, and defenseless man to pieces. — 1 Sam. xv. 33.

David had a plurality of wives and concubines; then lived an illegitimate life with the wife of Uriah; caused Uriah to be killed that he might continue his licentious debauchery; put his enemies under saws, axes and harrows, and burned them in brick-kilns. — 2 Sam. xi. 1, 6, 15; xii. 8, 29–31.

Solomon's crimes were so great and numerous, that even orthodox commentators feel a little shaky about holding him up for an example of purity. We should require a larger volume than this to record them.

Passing to the New Testament, we find matters not much improved. Jesus made mistakes, got angry with an audience because they could not answer a question, destroyed a drove of swine, cursed a fig-tree because it did not produce figs out of season, urged men to hate their wives and children, overthrew the tables belonging to money-changers, and by violence drove the Jews out of their own meeting-house. — Mark iii. 5; v. 13; Matt. xxi. 12, 19; Luke xiv. 26.

Peter denied his Lord, cursed and swore, quarreled with Paul, and lived after the manner of the Gentiles, at the same time compelling the Gentiles to live as do the Jews. — Matt. xxvi. 74; Gal. ii. 11–14.

Paul, by his own statement the "chief of sinners," became all things to all men, lied that the truth might abound, being crafty, caught his brethren with guile, and exhorted to obedience to bad laws. — 1 Cor. ix. 22; Rom. iii. 7; 2 Cor. xii. 16; Rom. xiii. 1, 2.

Such, dear reader, is a sample of the spots on the sun of Bible saints. Can Spiritualists exhibit a worse record? We now come directly to the question, Is Spiritualism in its phenomena and philosophy immoral? If immoral Spiritualists could be found in every village and hamlet in the world, it would no more prove Spiritualism immoral in its tendency than finding an immoral astronomer would prove astronomy immoral. Let it be understood that Spiritualism disfellowships no one on account of his doctrine or conduct. Believing that each one stands or falls to his own master, it is not our province to say who is or who is not worthy to hold communion with the inhabitants of the other world. If Jesus, while on earth, could talk with the Marys and Marthas (earth's Magdalenes), and say to the woman taken in the very act of adultery, "Neither do I condemn thee, go, and sin no more" (John viii. 11), why should the denizens of the spirit-world, who have themselves experienced earth's bitter trials, refuse to hold communion with those who most need it? Let an individual in the church commit a great crime, let him wallow in drunkenness in the mire, and there is not a church in christendom but that will disfellowship him. While they refuse to fellowship a person because of crime, ought there to be a sinner in the church? No. Then what is to become of the poor, church-forsaken sinner? He may wallow in the mire until he grows gray. The priest passes by on one side, and the Levite on the other; neither extending a helping hand, but each saying, "You miserable wretch! Go to hell for all of us; we will not have our church polluted with you. We came not to call sinners but the righteous to repentance." Spiritualism says, "Never was there a man so low but there was something good there. We must bless such." Hence, it welcomes such to its ranks. It is a reform school; and, if a person needs reforming either doctrinally or morally, he needs Spiritualism. Hence, their doctrines teach them to keep such in their ranks, and labor even more ardently for them than for those whose lives could be squared without it. Ho, ye vile, corrupt, polluted souls! Spiritualism calls. Extending its helping hand to you, it says, as Moses did to Hobab, "*Come and go with us, and we will do thee good.*" More would we give to see one poor, drunken sinner embrace Spiritualism than to see every evangelical Christian in the land flock to its standard, leaving poor outcasts in the cold. If the religious systems of the day can make their adherents good enough, they, perhaps, need no better; but, for heaven's sake, let Spiritualism live to bless those who are out of the reach of those who say, "Sit thou here, or stand thou there; for I am holier than thou."

Phenomenal Spiritualism teaches us that our friends whom we had supposed to be dead "are ever near us, though unseen." Is that immoral in its tendency? There is not a Spiritualist in the world who does not believe that he is surrounded by an angel brotherhood; that good, pure, and noble spirits are watching his every act, ever rejoicing in his good resolutions, and helping in his every effort to carry them into effect, and displeased, grieved, and chagrined with every wicked act. Spiritualists do not believe that they are ever alone. Fathers who have crossed death's "narrow stream," sainted mothers, angel wives, beautiful sons and daughters, all appeal with more than earthly logic and eloquence to the believer to "make strait paths for his feet." Will that belief make a man worse? Nay, tell us that noonday sun brings midnight darkness, that pure living water creates thirst, and that honey is bitter to the taste; but don't tell us that a belief that we are surrounded by the pure and good will incline us to evil.

Admit that Spiritualism is all false, that no spirit ever did or ever will communicate: is not the belief that they are around us, watching all our doings, and, perhaps, telling not only our doings, but our secret thoughts, to others (for Spiritualists believe that dead men tell tales sometimes), calculated to prompt us to watch our actions, words, and thoughts more closely than ever before? We so decide. We have had experience on each side of this great question, and, with the stake before us, we could not decide otherwise.

Are the dead with us? Do they watch our every act?

"How careful, then, ought I to live;
With what religious fear!"

Taking the above view of the subject, have not Spiritualists at least one stimulant to virtue not known to others?

If we turn from the phenomena to the philosophy taught by Spiritualism, we find that equally as urgently appealing to all there is of man to be true to his manhood. How is it with orthodoxy? There is not an evangelical church, or hardly a person who is a member of one, who does not indorse the sentiment that, —

"Between the stirrup and the ground,
Mercy was sought and pardon found."

If the foregoing couplet is not sung by them, they do sing that, —

> "While the lamp holds out to burn,
> The vilest sinner may return."

Can any thing be found in all heathenism as corrupting as the above couplet? It teaches the sinner to pursue his sinful course; "for as long as there is life there is hope." Where is there a person in all orthodoxy who does not believe that somehow, through the suffering of the innocent Nazarene, his guilty soul, all black with crime, will be washed and made white as the driven snow? The dying profligate offers a prayer, sheds a tear, and is immediately ushered into an upper-ten heaven, and, having taken advantage of the bankrupt law for sin, sits down by the side of the Great Jehovah as pure and good as the most sinless angel. Spiritualists do not believe this: they believe that all must suffer the consequence of their own actions.

> "There is no bankrupt law for sin,
> Though Pharisee may teach it;
> No limitation act steps in,
> Though Paul himself might preach it."

There is no "if," "and," or proviso in the matter; the violator of the law *can not escape:* he must in his own *proper person* suffer the penalty.

> "When you can tread on burning coals,
> And never scorch your feet,
> Then you may break God's righteous law,
> Its penalty not meet."

A familiar story will illustrate our ideas on this subject. It is said that in a distant country, almost nineteen centuries since, there were two individuals of directly opposite characters. One of them went about doing good, pronouncing benedictions on the poor, the sad, and the sorrowing. He made it his business to relieve all suffering under his control, whether moral, mental, spiritual, or physical. The other was a low, vile wretch, who made his living by highway robbery. In short, he was guilty of almost every crime in the calendar.

> "Now it happened that these men in their passing away
> From earth and its conflicts both died the same day."

These men were both assassinated at the same time; one on account of his crimes, the other in consequence of the prejudice of the people. While in the agonies of death, the murderer turned to the other, supposed by some to be a God, and said, "Lord, remember me when thou comest into thy kingdom." The other answered, "To-day shalt thou be with me in Paradise."

Now, we are led to ask, Is it so? Is it just? Did the thief go with Jesus to Paradise that day? If so, what is the difference, so far as the next world is concerned, whether a person is a Jesus or a thief? All have the same reward; the only difference being, one has gone into heaven honorably, while the other has taken advantage of a bankrupt law, and gone in on another's ticket.

Spiritualism does not teach that any person ever did or ever will go to heaven at the event called death.

It teaches that the only way to be in heaven when one passes from this sphere of existence is to *die in heaven*, and that the only way to die in heaven is to *live in heaven*, and that the only way to live in heaven is to *truly live, doing your duty toward every body and every thing*. Spiritualists believe that man will find what he carries, either in this or the other world; that he commences living in the other world where he left off here. If he dies a poor God-forsaken wretch, he will find himself such on the other side.

The poet sings, —

> "He wept that we might weep;
> Each sin demands a tear:
> In heaven alone no sin is found,
> And there's no weeping there."

But Spiritualism knows of no heaven where "no sin is found." It wants no such place. We ask, *we demand*, the privilege of sinning to all eternity. Do not mistake us. We do not want to sin; but we do want to prove to angels, to God, and last, though not least, to ourself, that we have no relish for sin: this we can only do by having the gates of sin thrown open, and the privilege of entering extended to us; then, if we refuse, all will know it is because we love the right. If, on the other hand, we are taken into the "heaven where no sin is found," and compelled to do right by a power *ab extra*, no credit is due us for our rectitude. We were only "the clay in the hands of the potter," the machine: if we run well, the builder, and not the machine, has the credit. With such an arrangement, Almighty God himself could not tell whether heaven was filled with angels or devils. Death makes man no better, no worse: each one finds himself, morally and spiritually, on the other side of its stream, where he left himself here. He opens his books where he closed them, commences living where he quit, finds himself surrounded with all the darkness and all the light in the summer-land that he has earned by his life here.

Our religion teaches us, not only that the consequences of our actions must be borne by ourselves, but that there is an *eternal* punishment for every sin, that every act of man makes its mark, that eternity is too short to wipe out the scars occasioned by sin. "Be sure your sin will find you out," is written in the Bible of the Spiritualist; and "Whatsoever a man soweth that shall he also reap," is as true to-day as in the first century.

This may be illustrated in the following manner. Two men at the age of forty have to-day passed to the spirit-world. One of them has spent his two-score of years in acquiring a physical, intellectual, moral, and spiritual education, and in living out the principles he has learned: the other has spent his forty years in drunken, carousing debauchery. He enters the spirit-world with his moral, mental, and spiritual faculties all blunted by his negligence and crime, insomuch that he does not realize that he has a spiritual nature. Perhaps it will take him as long after his passage to spirit-life, as he endured this, to wake up to consciousness enough to realize that he has thrown off the animal, and put on the spiritual body. He will learn sooner or later, by experience, if in no other way, that "though hand join in hand, the sinner can not go unpunished." In connection with this, he will soon see the necessity of progress. But, during the perhaps thrice forty years that he has been getting these lessons, his friend has been overcoming difficulties. Now he finds himself an almost immeasurable distance behind one by whose side he ought to stand. He never can reach his friend. After the most severe struggle, after years of incessant toil, he settles down with the humiliating reflection, "I am *so many* years behind one by whose side I should stand! Time will not help me to catch up: moments are graciously given, one comes as soon as another passes; and, though I improve them all, my friend does the same, and thus keeps his distance ahead of me."

Is not that an eternal punishment? Is it not punishment enough? Who would, who *could*, endure more?

Church systems teach that we are what God makes us: Spiritualism teaches that *we are what we make ourselves.* Patient reader, which of the two theories is the better calculated to urge its adherents forward to seek and put into practice the principles of harmony and truth? You are the juror. May we ask from you a candid and honest verdict?

That all may be led to see and put into *practical use* the pure principles which are being kindly vouchsafed to us by the angel-world, is the devout and earnest prayer of the writer of these pages.

CHAPTER III.

BIBLE DOCTRINE OF ANGEL MINISTRY.

A Common Doctrine — Angels are Spirits — Terms "Man" and "Angel" — Angel Men visit Abraham, Lot, Joshua — The Host of the Lord — An Angel appears to Gideon; to Manoah's wife; is introduced to Manoah — Writing on the Wall — Daniel a Superior Medium — Gabriel both a Man and Angel — The Stone rolled from the Sepulchre by a Man — Cornelius's Visitant — Peter a Trance-Medium — A Spirit talks to him — Peter's Explanation — The Book of Revelation a Series of Spirit-Communications — John sees his Brother — An Angel — God's Family — Bible replete with History of Angelic Ministration — No Bible-Writer has tried to prove it — All the Angels are Ministering Spirits — Number of Angels — Bible Saints trusted too much to the Angels — Abraham's Confidence — Angels select Isaac's Wife — "Murder will out" — Moses and the Angel — Angels deliver Israel — A Whole Nation of Mediums — Conditions must be obeyed — Joshua developed as a Medium — Joshua and the Angel — A Circle — Jericho taken — The *Modus Operandi* — Camels swallowed and Gnats rejected — Angel Ministry *vs.* Miracle — The Hebrews and the Fire — Nebuchadnezzar sees an Angel — Jugglers play with Fire — Chemicals prevent the Penetration of Heat — Letter from Rev. J. M. Peebles — The Explanation — The Result, an Increase of Faith — Master Frank Goodman — Mr. D. D. Home and the Fire Tests — Daniel and the Lions — Prayers answered by Angels — Jesus' Prayers — Daniel's Prayer — Angel's Effort to answer — Another finally assists and succeeds — The Emancipation Proclamation — An Ancient Prayer-Meeting — Peter let out of Prison — Peter at the Door — Only Spirit-Raps — Modern Mediums released from Prison — Author does not believe — Admonition.

"For he shall give his angels charge over thee, to keep thee in all thy ways." — Ps. xci. 11

THERE is, perhaps, not a Christian in the world who does not believe, that, in past ages, angels — ministering spirits — came from their heavenly abode to bless and assist the children of God. Tell churchmen that angels even now are watching over and blessing them, and they will tell you they always believed that. Have they not ever sung —

"There are angels hovering around"?

But when you inform them that God "maketh his angels spirits" (Ps. civ. 4), that they are all ministering spirits, sent forth to minister for them who shall be heirs of salvation (Heb. i. 14), some will shrink from you as though you were laden with a contagion which would sweep them from the earth. "What! my father and mother, my dead friends, come back? It is not possible!" Yes, it is possible; and we propose in this chapter to prove it. Not that we are going now to undertake to prove directly that spirits of the departed hold communion with earth's inhabitants: we have "rods in soak" on that question. We, in this chapter, design to show that "angels are spirits," and that they ever have and ever will administer to the inhabitants of earth. Perhaps our readers are not all of them aware that the terms "man" and "angel" are in the Bible used interchangeably with reference to those who have passed to the spirit-world. If not, a few references to that book will convince them that it is so. The three men who appeared to Abraham (Gen. xviii. 3) were none other than men whom we call dead.

In Gen. xix. 1, we read that two angels came to see Lot in Sodom; but verses 8, 9, 10, and 12, each state that they were men. Verse 15 again calls them angels; but, as if to forever seal the idea that men and angels are the same, verse 16 says, "The men laid hold upon his hand, and upon the hand of his wife, and upon the hand of his two daughters, the Lord being merciful unto them; and they brought them forth, and set them without the city."

In the heading of the fifth chapter of Joshua, we read, "An angel appeareth to Joshua;" but in verses 13, 14, instead of an angel appearing to Joshua, we have the following:—

"And it came to pass when Joshua was by Jericho, that he lifted up his eyes and looked, and, behold, there stood a *man* over against him, with his sword drawn in his hand; and Joshua went unto him, and said unto him, Art thou for us, or for our adversaries? And he said, Nay; but as captain of the host of the Lord am I now come. And Joshua fell on his face to the earth, and did worship, and said unto him, What saith my Lord to his servant?"

This man declares himself to be the "captain of the host of the Lord;" but the Lord's host is an angel host. See Gen. xxxii. 1, 2.

The "angel of the Lord" which came to Gideon in Judg. vi. 11, 12—that Gideon thought was a man, verse 22—is undoubtedly the spirit of the Lord, which came upon Gideon in verse 34, enabling him to use such wisdom, stratagem, and power in putting his enemies to flight.—Judg. vii. 19–21.

In Judg. xiii. 3, an angel of the Lord appeared to the wife of Manoah; but, when she related the matter to her husband, she said, "A man of God came unto me." In verse 8, Manoah prays for the man of God to come back. Verse 9 says, "God hearkened unto the prayer of Manoah, and the angel of God came to him; then the lady introduced the angel to her husband, calling him "the man of God;" after which Manoah and this man have a long *tête-à-tête*, in which this man is seven times called an angel.

In Dan. v. 5, it was not said to be the fingers of an angel's, but a *man's* hand, that wrote on the plaster of the wall of the king's palace. May we not reasonably suppose that this same man whose hand did the writing is the one who is called "the spirit of the holy gods," who influenced Daniel to interpret the writing? See verses 11, 14. Certain we are, that the spirit which influenced Daniel was said to be an excellent one (Dan. vi. 3); perhaps the same one who preserved Daniel's life, whom Daniel calls an angel, when he says, "My God hath sent his angel, and hath shut the lions' mouths" (verse 22). Daniel was evidently a medium, superior to any other in Babylon. It was for this reason that Nebuchadnezzar appointed Daniel "master of the magicians, astrologers, Chaldæans, and soothsayers; forasmuch as an excellent spirit and knowledge and understanding, interpreting of dreams, and showing of hard sentences, and dissolving of doubts, were found in the same Daniel." — Dan. v. 11, 12.

In Dan. viii. 13, one *saint* is heard talking to another. In verse 16, a man is heard talking to Gabriel, who is himself distinctly called a man (see Dan. viii. 21). The *manhood* of Gabriel does not in the least injure his *angelhood;* for we read in Luke i. 19, that "the *angel*, answering, said unto him, I am Gabriel that standeth in the presence of God."

In Matt. xxviii. 1–3, we have the account of the angel of the Lord descending from heaven, and rolling the stone back from the door of the sepulchre, and taking his seat on it. He is described as wearing raiment as white as snow, while his countenance was like the lightning. As this event occurred before daylight (see verse 1), it was a good time to exhibit spirit-lights; and perhaps that was what caused the illumination of his countenance. Matthew does not tell us who this angel was: but Mark does. He says, "And, entering into the sepulchre, they saw a young man sitting on the right side, clothed in a long, white garment; and they were affrighted." — Mark xvi. 5.

Cases similar to the above could be multiplied almost *ad infinitum;* but one more must suffice.

In Acts x. 1–8, we have the history of a devout man, one who "prayed to God alway." The writer of the Book of Acts says an angel came to him, and told him to send men to Joppa, to the house of one Simon a tanner, located on the sea-beach; and that he would find one Simon Peter, who had taken up lodgings with him; this Peter would tell him some things he ought to do. So he sent his servants as per order. Meanwhile, Peter went upon the house-top to pray: while in the act of prayer, he became entranced. (As some of our readers may not know what that means, we will invite them to visit a good trance-medium, and they will have its meaning ocularly demonstrated.) Strange visions were presented to Peter during this entrancement — visions which he did not understand: hence a *spirit* came to him to make an explanation. The spirit told him to go to the house, and find three men there who were seeking him, and go with them. From the tenor of this whole subject so far, we conclude that this spirit could have been none other than the angel who appeared to Cornelius. Peter followed spirit direction, and went to the house of Cornelius, and asked, "To what intent have you sent for me?" (verse 29.) Cornelius replied, "Four days ago I was fasting until this hour; and at the ninth hour, I prayed in my house, and, behold, a *man* stood before me in bright clothing," &c. (verse 30). Peter, upon witnessing the same phenomena among the Gentiles that he formerly had seen among the Jews, makes the discovery that "God is no respecter of persons;" and hence preached the gospel, and administered the ordinances to them, the same as though they had been Jews. Peter's Jewish brethren, of course, called him to an account for his innovation in preaching to the Gentiles; whereupon he tells his reasons for his course, the first of which was, "The spirit bade me go" (Acts xi. 12). The second was, when he got down there, Cornelius "showed us how he had seen an *angel* in his house, which stood and said unto him, Send men to Joppa, and call for one Simon, whose surname is Peter."—Acts xi. 13.

In this narrative we have, 1st, An *angel* appearing to Cornelius. 2d, This angel goes to Peter on the housetop, but is a *spirit* when he gets there. 3d, Cornelius, in relating the phenomenon which occurred in his house, says, A *man* appeared to me; and, 4th, When Peter rehearsed this matter to his Jewish brethren, he said, "Cornelius showed us how that he had seen an *angel*." Is not this enough to elucidate the fact that the terms "angel," "spirit," and "man," are used synonymously and interchangeably in the Bible? If not, we will favor our readers with one more evidence, drawn from the Book of Revelation.

The book known as the Apocalypse is but a communication, or rather series of communications, from a circle of seven spirits. (See Rev. i. 4.) We do not know who they all are. Daniel the prophet was probably one of them (see Rev. xix. 10, xxii. 7, 8); Jesus the Nazarene another (Rev. i. 5, xxii. 16). One of them was seen and very minutely described in Rev. i. 14–17. Others were seen several times, but not described so particularly. Seven times in this book, those who have ears to hear are admonished to "hear what the *spirit* saith unto the churches." Would that the churches even now were willing to heed the admonition to listen to spirit-voices!

In Rev. xxii. 8, John gets a view of one of the spirits through whom his book is being given; again his veneration is excited, and he is about to fall down and worship: but we will let him tell his own story.

"And I John saw these things, and heard them. And, when I had heard and seen, I fell down to worship before the feet of the *angel* which showed me these things. Then saith he unto me, See thou do it not; *for I am thy fellow-servant, and of thy brethren the prophets, and of them which keep the sayings* of this book: worship God." — Rev. xxii. 8.

From the array of testimony already presented, it would seem to be impossible to draw any other conclusion than that angels are inhabitants of the "summer-land," who were once earth's children, clothed in flesh and blood.

How glorious the truth that God has a family in heaven and upon earth! — Eph. iii. 15.

" One family, we dwell in Him,
One church above beneath,
Though now divided by the stream, —
The narrow stream of death.
One army of the living God,
To his command we bow;
Part of his host have crossed the flood,
And part are crossing now."

Not a member in heaven but that once inhabited earth, nor a member on earth who will not some day go to help make up the family in heaven.

" There are little feet I used to meet
When the world went well with me,
That I know will bound when the rippling sound
Of my boat comes over the sea."

Paul had a view of this when he said, —

" That in the dispensation of the fullness of times he might gather together in one *all things in Christ, both which are in heaven*, and which are on earth." — Eph. i. 10.

We will now advance to the more direct biblical evidences of angel ministry, and we may confess here that we do not know where to open the Bible; indeed, it makes but little difference where we open it. So replete is that book with the doctrine and history of the ministry of angels, that it would be hard work to open to the wrong page. We can not now think of a chapter that does not in some way include that doctrine. Yet not a Bible writer has ever undertaken to prove it: they have always referred to it in the most familiar manner, as though it were impossible that any one should ever have thought of disputing or questioning it. No writer in the Bible has ever undertaken to prove the existence of Deity. Moses commences his record by saying, "In the beginning, God created the heavens and the earth;" leaving us to infer his existence from the work he does: so they have always referred to angel ministry in the same way. Not a single occurrence is related as though the writer supposed he was telling any thing strange or new; but, on the other hand, every manifestation is told in such a style, with such an air of open frankness, that one would suppose that the writer supposed such occurrences so familiar, that one would almost as soon think of questioning his own existence as questioning such facts.

Paul's expression, "Are they not all ministering spirits, sent forth to minister for them who shall be heirs of salvation?" (Heb. i. 14,) is not an argument, but rather a reference to a universally-received sentiment, that not a part, but *all* the angels are ministering spirits. Is it so? Is every one who has passed to the "better land" an angel? and are *all the angels* ministering spirits? Then, by what a host are "earth-born souls" surrounded! Paul calls it, "*An innumerable company of angels*, . . . spirits of just men made perfect (Heb. xii. 22, 23). David calls the host, "Many thousands of angels" (Ps. lxviii. 17, *margin*). Moses represents these many thousand angels as being "ten thousand saints" (Deut. xxxiii. 2). Daniel and John each saw "*ten thousand* times ten *thousand* angels" (Dan. vii. 10; Rev. v. 11). Again: John saw a great company of angels, "which no man could number." These were redeemed from among the tribes of earth (Rev. vii. 9–16). An illustration of the number of angels which may surround and bless each individual may be found in the words of Jesus, "Thinkest thou that I can not now pray to my Father, and he shall presently give me more than twelve legions of angels?" (Matt. xxvi. 53.) The Assyrian army numbered more than one hundred and eighty-five thousand soldiers, for at least there were that many awoke one morning and found themselves all dead corpses (2 Kings xix. 35); yet Elisha the prophet was perfectly confident that the angels that surrounded him would outnumber the soldiers of the Assyrian army (2 Kings, vi. 16).

Our views upon this and kindred subjects, differing as they do from those called "orthodox," have been the cause of the world hailing us as "infidel" a great many times. Now, we care nothing for such charges, knowing that their malignity can only be equaled by their falsity. We never believed so much of the Bible, nor understood it so well, as to-day; and, though we are a Spiritualist from the crown of our head to the sole of our foot, our chief trouble with the Bible has been its unqualified indorsement of every thing spiritualistic. The writers of the Bible, and those who figured most largely in biblical history, placed entirely too much confidence in angel ministry. Not only did they depend upon their angel friends to do for them what they ought to have done for themselves, but they often put their own *individuality* aside, trusting their spirit-guides to do their *thinking* for them. The word with Israel's greatest men was, "Go and inquire of the

Lord." One of her greatest kings lost his life by his unswerving fidelity to what came to him from the spirit-world. (See 1 Kings xxii. 21–33.) A case in point may be found in Gen. xxiv. Abraham had become an old man, and knew that he must shortly pass away; of course, he felt a degree of solicitude about his son's marriage. What did he do but call his servant to him, and make him swear that he would go and bring his son a wife from the land of Canaan, assuring the servant that angels would pick her out? Hear his benediction as his servant is about starting: "The Lord God of heaven, which took me from my father's house, and from the land of my kindred, and which spake unto me, and that swear unto me, saying, Unto thy seed will I give this land: *he shall send his angel* before thee, and thou shalt take a wife unto my son from thence." — Gen. xxiv. 7.

The servant pursues his journey, consulting angels and getting tests, until, by a series of unmistakable signs, Rebekah was signified as the one to be Isaac's wife. Like a good girl, she goes along with the servant, whom probably she had never seen before, to marry a man whom she never had seen. Isaac took her as soon as the medium brought her to him, and went with her to keeping house in his mother's tent; and with one little exception, when he denied her (which may not have been from a lack of affinity, but from a hereditary disease, as his father had done the same thing), got along smoothly with her all his days.

Now, we frankly confess, that, as much of a Spiritualist as we are to-day, if we wanted a wife, we would not take her, "sight unseen," as boys trade jack-knives, even though an angel did pick her out. We would send no less or greater a personage than ourself after her every time. This, dear reader, was what we meant when we intimated that Bible people relied too much on the angel world.

To give the history of angelic manifestations among the Jews would be to record their entire national history. A few sketches must suffice to illustrate the matter.

Moses' first public act was to commit a murder. The next day after killing an Egyptian, he saw two of his Hebrew brethren in an altercation, and strove, as a good brother should, to create harmony; but the one in the fault said, —

"Who made thee a prince and a judge over us? Intendest thou to kill me, as thou killedst the Egyptian?" (Ex. ii. 14.) The old proverb, "Murder will out," proved true in this case; and, though Moses was heir to the throne of Egypt, he was compelled to flee his country for his life. He went to Midian, and fell in love with the daughter of a Midianitish priest, and married her, and engaged to act as shepherd, to take charge of his father-in-law's sheep. He took the sheep up into the mountains, and was not there very long, until his attention was attracted by a strange light, *a spirit-light*, such as thousands of Spiritualists have seen. He, of course, not having witnessed such phenomena before, was astonished to see such a fire in the bush, and the leaves remain green: so he turned aside to investigate the cause of this strange manifestation, when he discovered that there was an angel in the bush. By this time, Moses became clairaudient, and the angel enters into a conversation with him; finally, the whole scene winds up with sundry physical manifestations, by which Moses himself becomes convinced of his medium-power. — See Ex. iii., iv.

From this time forward, not a move was made toward the deliverance of the children of Israel, but that was made under spirit-direction. When the Hebrews became convinced that angels would go with them, and lead them through the wilderness, they started, and not until then. The angel went before them, in the daytime in a pillar of cloud, and at night in a pillar of fire (Ex. xiii. 21, xiv. 19, 20). When they failed to see the angel, they pitched their tents, and tarried until they had a new spirit-manifestation. The spirit-world seemed determined to develop a race of mediums: thus they led them round and round through the mountainous wilderness, for a period of *forty years*, to make a journey that could have been accomplished within forty days. The object was to develop a mediumship through which they could take the land and inherit it.

During this tedious tarrying in the wilderness, they are again and again promised assistance from the angel-world, and urged to yield the most strict obedience to their spirit-guides. One instance out of many we must record. In Ex. xxiii. 20–23, the Jehovah is represented as speaking to them as follows: —

"Behold, I send an angel before thee, to keep thee in the way, and to bring thee into the place which I have prepared. Beware of him, and obey his voice, provoke him not; for he will not pardon your transgressions: for my name is in him. But if thou shalt indeed obey his voice, and do all that I speak, then I will be an enemy unto thine enemies, and an adversary unto thine adversaries. For mine angel shall go before thee, and bring thee in unto the Amorites, and the Hittites, and the Perizzites, and the Canaanites, the Hivites, and the Jebusites; and I will cut them off."

Here the promise is very positive, "Obey the voice of the angel," comply with the conditions, and you shall conquer the inhabitants of the country where you are going. Fail in obedience, and you will fail to get possession. To carry these promises out, when Moses gets so old he is no longer fit to lead Israel, he ordains Joshua to the work. (See Num. xxvii. 18; Deut. xxxiv. 9.) They cross the Jordan, take the land, and conquer the nations, according to programme; all except the inhabitants of the city of Jericho. Of it the historian says, "Now the city of Jericho was straitly shut up because of the children of Israel: none went out, and none came in." — Josh. vi. 1.

Now the question arises, What can be done? Jericho was surrounded by its towering walls, and Israel had no battering-rams of sufficient power to batter them down, no machinery with which to throw "shot and shell" over the walls. How will they take the city? Joshua walked out one day, and suddenly became clairvoyant, and saw a *man* with a sword drawn in his hand. Joshua, supposing this man to be one yet in the flesh, says, "Art thou for us, or for our adversaries?"—"Nay," says the angel-man, "but as captain of the host of the Lord am I now come." He then proceeds to give Joshua the conditions upon which they can deliver the city into Israel's hands. The substance of the conditions is, that a circle must be formed around the city, which must last seven days: the implements of their religion must be carried with them. The fact is, the atmosphere must become thoroughly impregnated with the magnetism of that mediumistic nation in order to produce a tremendous physical demonstration of spiritual power. The programme was carried out, the people formed their circle, marched around the city, raised a tremendous shout, and the walls fell. Now, we ask, What brought them down? Did the people shout them down? No. If the walls fell at all, it was a physical manifestation of spirit-power. How strange that men will swallow such stories as are found in the fifth and sixth chapters of Joshua, and that without the slightest evidence, the record aside, that they are true, and at the same time utterly refuse to believe stories not a hundredth part as large, that come to us now backed by a hundred times the amount of testimony! However, we are happy to know that it is only in religious matters that people reject common sense. Now, there is not a particle of evidence that these things ever occurred (the evidence is all against it), yet men swallow it down without any scruples, and yet deny hundreds of well authenticated proofs that manifestations, *the same in kind*, though not in extent, occur every day in their own country and among their own neighbors.

Had we the space, and our readers the patience, to pursue this interesting subject *in extenso*, we would examine every so-called miracle in the Bible, and take the miracle out of it, and put angel ministry in its place. But time is precious: one or two instances must suffice.

We have often heard of the miracle of the three

young Hebrews being thrown into a furnace of fire, "made one seven times hotter than it was wont to be heated," and coming out without a hair of their heads being singed, or the smell of fire passing on their garments. The fact is, Nebuchadnezzar said he saw *four men* walking loose in the fire, "and they have no hurt on them, and the form of the fourth is like the Son of God" (Dan. iii. 25). It was a son of God, one of the very sons of God of whom Jesus spoke when he said, —

"But they which shall be accounted worthy to obtain that world, and the resurrection from the dead, neither marry nor are given in marriage, neither can they die any more; for they are equal unto the angels, *and are children of God*, being children of the resurrection." — Luke xx. 35, 36.

Nebuchadnezzar afterwards, instead of referring to this deliverance as a miracle, blessed God, "who hath sent his angel, and delivered his servants." — Dan. iii. 28.

Now, in all candor, we ask, Why not? Who has not seen jugglers put certain chemicals on their hands, and thus "quench the violence of fire"? We have. But all the chemicals used by these men are in the earth and its surroundings. May there not be chemists on the other side who have sufficient power to extract these elements, and envelop their mediums in a tissue of them, so refined, that heat can not penetrate it? We believe, yea, we *know*, that, under favorable conditions, it can be done.

Who of our readers has not seen or heard of Rev. J. M. Peebles, editor of the Western Department of "The Banner of Light"? We remember, when we were preaching Adventism, and he Spiritualism, in Battle

Creek, Mich., to have called on him one morning, (for we confess to have had a strange liking for him, even when we regarded him as the Devil's agent. We thought, "What a pity the Devil selects the best material in this world as his servants!") and he related the circumstance of having seen a man play with fire in such a wondrous manner, that had we not been a believer in the Bible, as well as in the veracity and intelligence of the speaker, we could not have credited it. We have written Mr. Peebles to give us the circumstance. His response is so direct and pointed, that we publish it entire.

HAMMONDTON, N.J., March 31, 1869.

REV. MOSES HULL.

Dear Friend, — Your favor of March 11 lies before me, with contents noted. I cheerfully comply with the request to furnish you a brief statement of a remarkable spiritual manifestation witnessed by myself through the mediumship of Dr. E. C. Dunn, involving a seeming suspension of the laws connected with heat.

These are the main facts:

My friend Dr. Dunn, accompanying me several years on my lecture tours as a healing medium, speaking occasionally under spirit-control, was often entranced in my presence. Our electric atmospheres naturally intermingling, the magnetic sympathy became finally so intensified, that a portion of my circle of spirits could quite easily throw the doctor into an unconscious trance condition.

One of these spirit-guides — a thinker and practical chemist on earth — was Perasee Lendanta, living in the mediæval ages, and equally conversant with the Christian and Neoplatonic dogmas. Whenever he entranced the doctor, I expected a feast of reason and flow of sound thought.

At the close of a service in Battle Creek, Mich., on a Sunday of June, 1862, inviting and even urging the doctor, he accompanied me home. Soon, while comfortably sitting in my library-room, he became suddenly entranced, and, during the entrancement, this *conversation*, with the manifestation, followed: —

"Owing to the good conditions to-day," said the spirit, "I was enabled to approach very near you while lecturing; thus infusing much of my own force and thought into your discourse."

"Thank you. I felt your presence. You are to me like a wall of fire and a shield of brass, imparting a stern, positive, independent feeling."

"The world has yet to learn the full import of the terms 'individualism,' 'self-reliance,' 'independence.' . . . What inquiries to-day?"

"I desire to ask this question: Were Shadrach, Meshach, and Abednego cast into a fiery furnace, coming out with not a hair of their 'heads singed,' nor the 'smell of fire' upon them?"

"I don't know, sir. Was not there."

"Well, do you believe the recorded scriptural account?"

"Most certainly, I do."

"Why do you believe it?"

"In the first place, because *reasonable*, and, in the second place, because the same and even more remarkable things may be done in the present."

"If so (half smiling, half doubting), I should like to see a slight practical illustration of your position."

"If you have a large kerosene-lamp in your house, procure, light, and place it before this medium, with the blaze on, high as it will bear."

Securing the lamp, and placing it before the doctor in full blaze, this controlling spirit thrust the medium's hand into it, holding it there full *five minutes;* the flames streaming up between the fingers. It seemed as though it must be burned to a crisp. Finally, the spirit-intelligence removing it, I wiped the smoke and soot from the hand, and it was not in the least injured by the fire. After a little spasmodic struggling, as usual, the medium became conscious, complaining only of a terrible magnetic pressure upon his head. This soon wore away, when, before leaving the room, he was again entranced.

"There!" said the spirit, "you have seen a man's hand thrust into the fire, and not burned."

"Certainly, I have: now tell me how you did it."

"Owing to the feebleness of the English language in the line of metaphysics and spiritual science, this would be a more difficult task than to seemingly destroy the law of heat. I will try. Aided by others, I gathered or accreted fine, etherealized spirit-substances from surrounding spirit-space, and, polarizing and otherwise preparing them, constructed a sort of electric coating or covering, winding it close around the medium's hand. This covering was just as impervious to heat as is a pane of glass to the beating rain-drops. Furthermore, I could envelop this whole mortal form in this magnetic mantle; and, so long as I could maintain the requisite conditions, the body would not be injured by fire.

"Something very similar is evidenced in the case of the three men cast into the *fiery furnace*. It was an ancient spiritual manifestation. Your Scriptures say, 'Lo, I see four men loose walking in the midst of the fire; . . . and the form of the fourth is like the Son of God.' This '*fourth*,' seen by the clairvoyant eye, was an angel, or spiritual being that once inhabited your or some other earth in the universe of the infinite."

This circle of spirits has given me other manifestations more wonderful than the above, paralleling those of biblical times. Thus the past and present are made to unite in their testimony of spirit manifestation and communion. I have a more clear, logical faith to-day in those *visions*, *dreams*, *prophecies*, *healings*, *trances*, and other wonderful manifestations recorded in the Jewish and Christian Scriptures, than when wearing my clerical robes. And the partially "*hushed*" *infidelity* of Presbyterian, Baptist, Methodist, Universalist, and Second-Advent Christians, is to me absolutely shocking. By the "grace of God," let us, Brother Hull (aided by the sweet fellowship of angels), continue to pray and to labor for the enlightenment and salvation of those Christians whose impudence is only excelled by their deplorable ignorance of natural law, spiritual science, and the watchful presence of God's ministering spirits.

Most truly thine,

J. M. Peebles.

After such evidence, from such a source, it would seem that nothing further is necessary; yet we find it hard to resist the temptation to present other evidences.

In a late number of "The American Spiritualist,"

we find a lengthy communication from A. Goodman of Columbus, O., giving the history of the mediumship of Master Frank Goodman, a lad of eleven summers. Mr. Goodman says, —

"Next came showing, touching, and shaking of hands; playing on guitar; and raising Frank to the ceiling. All this was done in daylight, except the raising of the medium; that, with the showing of phosphoric lights, requiring darkness. Now, in conclusion, I will only add a few of many equally wonderful manifestations, given since our return to this place. One is the fire-test, in which the medium, while entranced, handles red-hot coals, without the slightest injury; also thrusts his head into the grate among the flames, without a hair being singed. Another is the ring-test. The spirits having made the request, I obtained five copper rings, of different sizes, which Frank keeps with other articles in a small tin box. One day recently, while out on the street, all these rings were put upon his arms and legs, under all his clothing, without his knowledge: and he was obliged to wear them for a week; for, in trying to remove one of them, I gave him so much pain, that I had to give it up. They were taken off by the spirits as quietly as they were put on."

The writer concludes his article by saying, —

"Any one desiring further information with regard to the same is at liberty to address the writer, or to visit us in person."

Will our skeptical readers avail themselves of this privilege? It may help them to arrive at a knowledge of the truth.

A London correspondent of "The New-York Times,"

in speaking of Mr. D. D. Home and his mediumship, says, —

"He was carried horizontally out of a window in the third story of the house of Lord ——, and brought in at the window of another room, some thirty feet distant; having been carried through the air forty feet or more from the ground. Finally, he has on several occasions taken a large live coal from a coal-fire, held it in his hand, and laid it in the hands of other persons, without even the smell of fire or the sensation of heat being perceived by them. My informant showed us where his own finger had been burnt in testing the value of this manifestation. He assured me that he had seen Mr. Home go to a large coal-fire, and lay his face upon the white-hot coals, without singeing his hair or beard. As this is a pretty strong story, I beg to append the following, which I find in 'The Spiritual Magazine' for this month. Mr. Hall is the well-known editor of 'The Art Journal;' his wife, Mrs. S. C. Hall, is well known as a writer, and has lately received a pension from the queen.

15 Ashley Place, Victoria Street, S.W.

Sir, — I state facts without explanation or comment. On the 27th of December, I was sitting, with nine other persons, in my drawing-room. Mr. D. D. Home left the table, went to a bright fire, took thence a lump of living coal, brought it red to the table, and placed it on my head. Not a hair was singed, nor did I sustain any injury. The coal remained upon my head about a minute. Mr. Home then took it, and placed it in Mrs. Hall's hand, without injury to her; and he afterwards placed it in the hands of two of our guests. The gas-light and two candles were burning in the room. I add that the nine other persons present would depose to these facts. Your obedient servant,

S. C. HALL.

"The editor adds the following note: 'At the conference at Lawson's Rooms, Jan. 14, Mr. H. D. Jenckin publicly stated the facts here given by Mr. Hall, and added several instances of the kind which he had witnessed. The fire-test, he said, had now been seen by more than fifty persons in the metropolis and its neighborhood.'"

Epes Sargent, in his "Despair of Science," says, —

"At a *séance* in London, in 1860, in the presence of several persons (whose names are at the service of the curious), Mr. Home, being entranced, did, in the presence of all, lay his head on the burning coals; where it remained several moments, he sustaining no injury: not a hair of his head was singed." — Pp. 97, 98.

We have already referred to the so-called miracle of the deliverance of Daniel from the hungry lions; but it was only a physical manifestation of spirit-power. Daniel says, —

"My God hath sent his angel, and hath shut the lions' mouths, that they have not hurt me; forasmuch as before him innocency was found in me; and also before thee, O king, have I done no hurt." — Dan. vi. 22.

While we have strong confidence in prayer, fully believing that prayers are heard and answered, we do not believe that God has any other way of answering prayer but by virtue of angel ministry. It was an angel that administered to Jesus in the Garden of Gethsemane, when, in the bitterness of his soul, he prayed, "Father, if it be possible, let this cup pass from me" (Luke xxii. 43). He could pray to his Father, and, as a result, have more than twelve legions of angels to assist him (Matt. xxvi. 53). It was in answer to prayer, that the angel came to Cornelius (Acts x. 1). In Daniel, chapters ix. and x., we have a very full history of the prophet's three weeks' prayer and fasting. At the end of this time, "a certain *man* clothed in linen," whom Daniel describes very minutely, came to him; spirit hands touched him; "one like the similitude of the sons of men" opened his mouth, and enabled him to speak. There were other parties with Daniel, who were not sufficiently developed to see; yet "great quaking fell upon them." This man, or angel, that came to Daniel, informed him that his prayers were heard long ago; but the prince of the kingdom of Persia withstood him twenty-one days, that is, just three weeks, exactly the length of time Daniel was praying (compare verses 2, 3, with 12, 13, of Dan. x.); after which, says the angel, "Michael, one of the chief princes, came to help me." This Prince Michael is prince among the angels (see Jude 9; Dan. ix. 21). The two, Michael and this other angel-man, succeeded in working upon the prince of the kingdom of Persia: so that Daniel's prayer was answered. The emancipation proclamation was written and sent out by the prince of the kingdom of Persia, and Israel was again free.

A very important case of the answer to prayer by angels is found in Acts xii. 4–16. The case is so interesting, we give it entire.

"And, when he had apprehended him, he put him

in prison, and delivered him to four quaternions of soldiers to keep him; intending, after Easter, to bring him forth to the people. Peter, therefore, was kept in prison; but prayer was made without ceasing of the church unto God for him. And when Herod would have brought him forth, the same night Peter was sleeping between two soldiers, bound with two chains: and the keepers before the door kept the prison. And, behold, the angel of the Lord came upon him, and a light shined in the prison; and he smote Peter on the side, and raised him up, saying, Arise up quickly. And his chains fell off from his hands. And the angel said unto him, Gird thyself, and bind on thy sandals; and so he did. And he saith unto him, Cast thy garment about thee, and follow me. And he went out, and followed him, and wist not that it was true which was done by the angel; but thought he saw a vision. When they were past the first and the second ward, they came unto the iron gate that leadeth unto the city, which opened to them of his own accord; and they went out, and passed on through one street; and forthwith the angel departed from him. And when Peter was come to himself, he said, Now I know of a surety, that the Lord hath sent his angel, and hath delivered me out of the hand of Herod, and from all the expectation of the people of the Jews. And when he had considered the thing, he came to the house of Mary the mother of John, whose surname was Mark, where many were gathered together praying. And as Peter knocked at the door of the gate, a damsel came to hearken, named Rhoda. And when she knew Peter's voice, she opened not the gate for gladness, but ran in, and told how Peter stood before the gate. And they said unto her, Thou art mad. But she constantly affirmed that it was even so. Then said they, It is his angel. But Peter continued knocking: and when they had opened the door, and saw him, they were astonished."

A similar case is found in Acts v. 19–26. We can not take up any sentence of this lengthy paragraph and elucidate it. We see nothing inconsistent or miraculous in the transaction. The soldiers were, doubtless, thrown into a sound magnetic sleep. The light which shone in the prison was a spirit-light, such as our own eyes have beheld on several occasions. The doors did not, as Peter supposed, open of their own accord: Peter was not sufficiently clairvoyant to see the angel who unlocked them, and swung them back on their hinges. How natural that he should go to the house of Mary! there was a magnet there; there it was that his brethren were assembled for prayers, and angels were collected. When the "raps" were heard at the door, how natural that little Rhoda should be the one who should open it, and, in her joy exclaim, "It's Peter, it's Peter!" But the church had not witnessed enough of the phenomena to be fully convinced: so their first conclusion was, "The damsel is mad," the girl is insane. Soon, however, they change their mind, and conclude that the raps are only spirit-raps: hence they assert, "It is his angel."

Now, we are frank to acknowledge that we believe the whole circumstance. We have seen things so similar, that we should be untrue to ourself to deny this. The same law which produces such things now could have produced them then.

Mr. Rand and the Davenport brothers were once imprisoned in the common jail of the city of Oswego, N.Y., for the crime of demonstrating immortality, without taking out a juggler's license. Mr. Rand himself tells the story of his release; from it we extract the following: —

"They were informed by the spirits that the prison-doors would be opened before their time expired; and, in the evening previous to its expiration, a voice spoke in the room, and said that I was to go out that night. I was told to put on my coat and hat, and be ready. It was oppressively warm in our small room, with the window and door both closed; and I asked if I could be allowed to sit with my coat off, as I did not expect we should be released for more than an hour; but the answer was, 'Put on thy coat and hat. Be ready.' I did so, not even then supposing we should be released until the jailer and his family had retired, and all might be still without. But I was disappointed. Immediately, not probably twenty minutes from the time we were locked up, the door was thrown open; and the voice again spoke, and said, 'Now go quickly. Take with you the rope (for a rope had been in our room, which had been used for another purpose in our former room, as we have previously said), go to yonder garret-window, and let thyself down, and flee from this place. We will take care of the boys. There are many angels present, though but one speaks.' I hastily passed on, and strictly obeyed the angel. The boys came out with me into the hall, took up the lock which lay upon the floor, and for the first time examined it: spoke of its being warm. The angel told them, as they subsequently informed me, to go into the room again; and the door was closed and locked again by the angel, and they were to remain there for the night."—*History of Davenports, by Rev. Orrin Abbott*, p. 70.

The above case we have investigated quite thoroughly. We know, that, so far as human testimony is concerned, its truth is established beyond a reasonable doubt. Other cases of the same kind have occurred within our knowledge; then, why should we deny such things when found in the Bible?

Now, shall we say we believe in angel ministry? We can not. Taking all these biblical evidences, together with the modern phenomena, including what our eyes have seen and our ears have heard, we can not believe, *we know*, "angels are ministering spirits."

"They come, and night is no more night,
Pale sorrow's reign is o'er;
And death is but the gate of light,
And gloomy now no more."

We have been too often blessed, advised, protected, defended, delivered, and *saved* by them, to entertain doubts on the subject. We know the angels have taken us out of the hands of ferocious mobs. We know that they are always present, that the thoughts we now pen are influxes from the spirit-world. Angels are even now in the room.

"How cheering the thought that the spirits in bliss
Do bow their bright wings to a world such as this,
Do leave their bright home in the mansions above
To breathe o'er our spirits some message of love!"

Dear reader, would you *know* of this divine communion? Would you enjoy the society of an angel brotherhood? Would you be led in green pastures, beside the still waters? Would you drink from the never-failing fountain of inspiration? Then place yourself in a condition where you can enjoy communion with your "elder brethren." It will open to your soul fountains of happiness the world can know nothing of. That readers and writer may ever be led into the paths of truth and righteousness, and be accounted worthy, even during this life, to associate with the inhabitants of the angel-world, is our most devout and humble prayer.

CHAPTER IV.

THE THREE PILLARS OF SPIRITUALISM.

Spiritual Platform — Three Propositions — Man has a Spiritual Nature — Spirit not immaterial — Spiritual Man — Source of Evidence — Biblical Testimony — Elihu — Zephaniah — Papal Decree — Hard Questions — Can not answer all — Spiritual Senses — Blind and Deaf Man — Illustration — Man Double — Two Fathers — Two Sources of Knowledge — Peter awakened — Two Contradictory Histories of Jesus — Both true — Jesus did not always believe his own Prophecies — Somnambulism an Important Witness — Author's Case — A Lady and the Fine Arts — Dr. Slade and Spirit Pictures — The *modus operandi* — Psychometry — Discourses read from the Hand, the Walls of the House, &c. — Paul's Case — Outward and Inward Man — One perishes, the other endures — Modern Facts — Apparitions of the Living — Mrs. Hauffe — Lady in Albany — Apparition at St. Louis — Hiram Dayton badly mixed — His Father appears — Case in New Orleans — Drowning Persons — Spirit continues after the Death of the Body — Spirit a Conscious Entity — Spirits in Prison — Gospel preached to the Dead — Spirits return — Modern Spiritualism a Repetition of that of the Bible — Samuel and Saul — No Devil or Witch in the Case — Josephus's Testimony — Character of the Woman — Moses and Elias — "Only a Vision" — Various Phases of Manifestation — Child Medium — Written Communication from Elijah the Prophet — Belshazzar's Palace Wall — Elias must come — John the Baptist a Medium — This was Elias — "He hath a Devil" — Ezekiel's Mediumship — Saul a Medium — An Evil Spirit visits him — Modern Evidences — Dr. Johnson's Testimony — Vision of a French Marquis — Prediction fulfilled — Testimony Conclusive.

PERHAPS we have pursued our investigation far enough to hand to our readers a *platform* upon which Spiritualism rests. As we now have the "ball" fairly opened, we may as well proceed to lay down a *digest* of some of the main evidences of Spiritualism, more especially those upon which we as an individual predicate our faith.

The "holy trinity" upon which Spiritualism is built, with which it stands or falls, and which must be attacked by opponents who would inaugurate an honorable warfare upon it, can be represented in the following sentences: —

1. *Man has a spiritual nature.*

2. *That spiritual nature exists and retains its consciousness after the dissolution of the body.*

3. *That spiritual nature, after it leaves the body, can come en rapport with and communicate to those yet in the flesh.*

All must see that with these propositions Spiritualism meets its fate. Take any one of them fairly away from Spiritualism, and upon its banners you write, "Thou art weighed in a balance and found wanting." On the other hand, with the sustaining of this trinity, Spiritualism becomes a *tri-unity*, a "threefold cord," which a wise man has said "is not easily broken." With the sustaining of these three propositions, Spiritualism becomes a citadel of strength, so fortified that its enemies can do but little more than to pick at its microscopic crudities and irregularities. Then let us turn our attention at once to their proof.

Man has a Spiritual Nature.

By this proposition we do not mean that man has an *immaterial* nature. The word "immaterial" has so long been connected with "spiritual," that the world has come to consider them synonymous. Yet one stands opposed to *animal;* while the other can be better represented by the word "nothing" than any other in the English language. That which is material is something; that which is the opposite of material is *im*material; that which is the opposite of something is nothing: hence *that which is immaterial is nothing.* This being true, those who take the position that spirit is immaterial deny its existence.

By the term "spiritual" we mean what the ancient Greeks meant by the term *pneumatikon;* that is, not animal, not corporeal, a nature not comprehended through the external organs of sense.

As we hold to no theory but that we can prove, either with or without the Bible, we will on this subject draw our first proofs from that book; not that they are true because they are in the Bible, but they are there because those who placed them there regarded them as true. There are thousands in the world to-day who would not dare to say their souls were their own, unless their Bible told them so; who would only require one "Thus saith the Scripture," to convince them that a man was older than his father; that the sun stood still about twelve hours while a Hebrew general marched his army several hundred miles, and fought six battles; that a man caught three hundred foxes, and turned tail to tail, and tied firebrands between them, and by that means burned down thousands of acres of his neighbor's green corn; that a whale got down into the Mediterranean Sea and swallowed a man; that after a three-days residence in the stomach of a great fish, during which time Jonah graduated, and prepared for the ministry, he entered unharmed upon his calling, went as a missionary to Nineveh, and proved himself divinely called, by uttering predictions which never were fulfilled that fire refused to burn certain Jews; and that sundry miracles were wrought by the Man of Nazareth on purpose to convince the people of his divinity, and yet the divine decree had gone forth, that, "seeing, they should see and not perceive, and, hearing, they should hear and not understand." For the benefit of such, we will first exhibit a sample of the biblical evidences that man has a spiritual nature.

The prophet Elihu has introduced this subject in the following unmistakable language: —

"There is a spirit in man; and the inspiration of the Almighty giveth them understanding." — Job xxxii. 8.

A more positive declaration of spiritualistic faith could not be made by the most sanguine Spiritualist; nor is this an isolated proof of this position. The Bible abounds in declarations as positive as the above. Zechariah, another of Israel's prophets, said, —

"The Lord . . . formeth the spirit of man within him." — Zech. xii. 1.

In this declaration, we not only have the assertion that man has a spirit, but that it is *formed*, *shaped*.

Pope Leo X. decreed that "the spirit is the same form as the body." We do not doubt that this decree of the infallible head of the Church is true, not, however, because it was decreed, any more than the rising of the sun to-morrow morning would be the result of a decree of his papal Majesty.

When we get thus far with our subject, we know that some of our readers who do not comprehend spiritual things are ready with a legion of questions concerning man's spiritual nature. May we confess right here, that, probably, we can not answer your questions? That, however, neither proves our theory untrue, nor our incompetency to rationally reason upon it. Paul says, —

"But the natural man receiveth not the things of the Spirit of God; for they are foolishness unto him: neither can he know them, because they are spiritually discerned. But he that is spiritual judgeth all things; yet he himself is judged of no man." — 1 Cor. ii. 14, 15.

From this we learn that it is impossible for him whose spiritual faculties have not been aroused to understand spiritual things. "*Neither can he know them.*" Then, why should we try to make him comprehend them? While we can not explain spiritual things to the "natural man" (and the spiritual man needs no explanation: he gets his knowledge of these things by intuition, not by tuition), we may be able to call his attention to phenomenal evidences which may convince him, that, though he can not understand them, they may, nevertheless, be true. We can not explain how light passes through a pane of glass without either glass or light being disorganized, yet we can any day, and in any house, point to such phenomena. We can not make the man who was born without eyes understand the difference between red, white, and blue; yet we can make him know that we see a difference which is not tangible to his senses. Discourse sweetest music to a totally deaf man, until the last hair on your head turns gray, and you can not make him comprehend that there is an interval of a fifth between C and G.

We said, and have set out to prove, that man has a spiritual nature. We now assert that man is *double;* he has a *duplex entity.* If Paul understood this question, we all have two fathers. His language is, —

"Furthermore, we have had fathers of our flesh, which corrected us; and we gave them reverence: shall we not much rather be in subjection to the Father of spirits, and live?" — Heb. xii. 9.

This passage deserves more than a cursory notice. Paul says, "We have had *fathers* (plural) of our flesh; and we gave them (plural) reverence: shall we not much rather be in subjection to the *Father* (singular) of spirits (plural), and live?" By this we see that though there may be as many fathers of the flesh of our readers as there are readers, yet their spirits all have the same father. This father is God, who is a spirit. — John iv. 24; Acts xvii. 29.

Man, having two fathers, might reasonably be expected to have two natures, sometimes called two men (see 2 Cor. iv. 16). There are two sources whence men get knowledge. Some things we learn by aid of our five senses; some things we know independent of the organs of sense.

Jesus once said to Peter, "that he must go to Jerusalem, and suffer many things of the elders, chief priests, and scribes, and be killed." But Peter did not believe it. He rebuked his Master, and said, "Be it far from thee, Lord: this shall not be unto thee." Whereupon, Jesus says, "Get thee behind me, Satan: thou art an offense unto me; for thou savorest not the things that be of God, but those that be of men." — See Matt. xvi. 21–23.

What other idea can any one glean from this than that Peter was not in a spiritual condition? he could understand the things that came to his fleshly senses from flesh and blood; other things he could not understand. But Peter's spiritual senses are not always asleep. On another occasion, Jesus asks him, "Whom do men say that I the Son of man am?" Peter answered, "Some say that thou art John the Baptist; some, Elias; and others, Jeremias, or one of the prophets." Then Jesus put the question directly to his disciples, "Whom do ye say that I am?" Peter says, "Thou art the Christ, the son of the living God." Jesus responds, "Blessed art thou, Simon Bar-jona; *for flesh and blood hath not revealed this to thee*, but my Father which is in heaven." — Matt. xvi. 13–17.

Who wonders that Jesus calls him blessed? He was in a condition where he was receiving knowledge independent of fleshly organs. He was not indebted even to his own fleshly eyes and ears for that revelation.

The two paragraphs above quoted show very plainly that at one time Peter was in a condition that he was not in at another. Once he "savored not the things of God;" at another time was receiving knowledge not from flesh and blood, but directly from the Father in heaven. Such is the history of all spiritually-minded persons; sometimes they seem so infilled with the spirit that all space and time are annihilated. The past is brought up with peculiar distinctness, and "coming events cast their shadows before." They see through solid walls, and at a distance, the same as though there was nothing to obstruct the vision. At other times, the animal man holds the dominion, and they, the same as others, view events from a material standpoint. At such times, they not unfrequently disbelieve what their own spiritual senses have told them; and many dispute what they, in the moments of their illumination, so clearly saw, that they could have pledged their own existence on its reality. It was so with Jesus: at times, his spirit seemed to reach out and grasp the future, so that he could say, "The Son of man shall be betrayed into the hands of men, and be crucified." At other times, he did not believe his own predictions, and he would promise his disciples that they should have a hundred times the amount of real estate in this world, for following him, that they could get by any other means; that they should sit on twelve thrones, judging the twelve tribes of Israel; that they should not taste of death till they should see his kingdom established with power. He even went so far on one occasion as to take the kingdom by violent force; but he saw his mistake afterward, and wept over it. — See Mark x. 29, 30; Matt. xix. 28, xvi. 28, xxi. 9–13, xxiii. 37–39.

Somnambulism is an important witness to the double entity of man. Its facts are so patent, that, perhaps, there is not one who will read this volume who will not remember having heard of persons getting up in their sleep, and performing wonderful feats of physical or mental strength. At the age of fourteen years, we were employed to carry shingles upon a three-story brick house; and several persons now living will testify, that, after the first day's work, we got up in our sleep in the night and took a bunch of white-wood shingles, perhaps five hundred, and carried them up on the house. Half of the number would have been more than we could have carried in our normal condition. When told of it the next morning, though we had been in the habit of sleep-walking ever since we were three years old, we could hardly believe the report of the witnesses; and we have never, from that day to this, been able to gather the faintest recollection of even dreaming of carrying shingles that night.

We remember to have read somewhere of a lady getting up in her sleep, and, in that condition, painting a picture, which, as a work of art, could not be excelled by the best artists in Europe. This lady was surprised, when admiring the painting the next day, to learn that she herself was its author; that she had done in a few hours, in a state of sound sleep, what she could by no possibility accomplish in her waking hours.

We know that Dr. Henry Slade of Jackson, Mich., when in an unconscious magnetic trance, has, in one hour, produced an exact life-size likeness of his wife, which, as a work of art, could not be excelled on this continent. The picture is in existence to-day, and more than a thousand witnesses in Michigan and New York can testify that the representation is true to life.

How are these things done? We have but one answer. "There is a natural body, and there is a spiritual body." One or the other of those bodies must hold the positive dominion. Ordinarily, in perfect physical health, the animal man is positive. "But, though the outward man perish, the inward man is renewed day by day." As the outward man loses strength, the spiritual, or inward man becomes positive: hence, if the physical man can be put into a perfectly sound sleep, it will be in a perfectly negative condition; then if the spiritual man can take the physical while asleep, and use it without awaking it, it can certainly control it better than it could when the physical was positive. So with mediumship: an organism that can be put into a sound magnetic sleep, and then used by a spirit-power, without being disturbed or awakened, will always make a good medium.

Psychometry might be presented as another evidence that man has a spiritual nature. We all have senses that we little dream of. Even dumb animals manifest powers which our positive intellectuality prevents many men and women from knowing they possess. The dog tracks the hare or fox with unerring certainty: so he will distinguish his master's track from that of ten thousand other men, by the *peculiar kind* of caloric his master throws off. Every individual is surrounded by a *magnetic aura* peculiar to him or her self: that we read often, without knowing it. Who has not often, upon being introduced to persons, formed an attachment, or taken a dislike, that no future acquaintance could change? Why was it? We answer, "The spirits, unknown, it may be, to the physical organism, sought and obtained an introduction to each other. They saw an affinity, or lack of it, as the case might be, that may require the bodies many months to learn." We have on several occasions met entire strangers, and recognized them by this magnetic atmosphere. We could not tell how we knew them, yet we were as positive who and what they were before as after a formal introduction. "How do you tell?" said a gentleman to us whom we called by name, never having seen him before. "By my feelings," was our response. "It is the most ridiculous nonsense," ejaculated our interrogator. "The natural man receiveth not the things of the spirit, *neither can he know them; they are foolishness unto him*," was our reply.

Though we never yet took a manuscript into an audience, we have not, in almost seventeen years' constant preaching, delivered as much as one discourse that we did not read. When we get up to speak, we can not look where our discourse is not; we can see it photographed on the walls of the room; we can read it in the countenances of our audience, or in our bare hand, or hear it in the very silence of the room, in pauses between our words.

Of these phenomena we could not even attempt an explanation: all we can say is, there is a spiritual world, and man is endowed with spiritual senses, which occasionally get a glimpse of what is behind the curtain of gross materiality.

We could weary the reader with volumes of such evidences as have been here presented. Indeed, it is more trouble to cease than to write; but we must approach the more direct evidence of the duplex entity of man.

The great apostle to the Gentiles relates an historical fact bearing directly upon this point. He says, "I knew a man in Christ above fourteen years ago, *whether in the body or out of the body I can not tell;* God knoweth; such an one caught up to the third heaven, . . . and heard unspeakable words, which it is not lawful [possible] for man to utter." — 2 Cor. xii. 2–4.

From this emphatic declaration of the learned Paul, we learn that he supposed it possible for a man to exist out of the body. Had man been all body, as certain ones suppose, and Paul understood it so, he never could have used the language, "Whether in the body or out of the body I can not tell." Again: the fact that words were heard which could not be uttered by corporeal organs of speech is proof abundant, not only that there is a language that fleshly lips can not speak, but that the man which exists sometimes in the body and sometimes out of it can hear when out of the body.

The spiritual nature, upon the existence of which depends the proof of Spiritualism, is, by Paul, referred to as follows: —

"For which cause we faint not; but though our outward man perish, yet the inward man is renewed day by day." — 2 Cor. iv. 16.

The inward man is certainly not the corporeal or animal man; for one man of that kind does not dwell within another. Although we are getting ahead of our subject, we must be permitted to say, that this text is a most positive proof of our second proposition, viz., that the spiritual nature exists and retains its consciousness after the body is dead. The outward man perish, and the inward man renewed? What can be plainer? Again: when the inward man is out of the body, from the fact of its having perished, or from any other cause, it hears unspeakable words, — words unuttered by fleshly lips. Could we have the framing of testimony to our liking, we could not make the matter more plain than Paul has done in these two instances.

But, to come to more modern facts, who has not read and heard and known of instances of persons leaving the body, even here in this life, and appearing, sometimes at a distance of hundreds of miles from it; thus giving proof of their double entity?

Take the case related by Capt. Robert Bruce, of the man on the wrecked vessel appearing at the same time on another vessel, several leagues distant, and writing on the captain's slate, "Steer to the nor'west." Mr. Bruce himself saw the man write; others saw the writing. They steered as directed, and saved the lives of a crew by doing so. The man who did the writing, it appeared afterward, by a comparison of the notes of the two sea-captains, was in a trance at the time it was done.

If the reader will take the trouble to take the book called "Footfalls on the Boundaries of Another World," by Hon. Robert Dale Owen, and read any two or three of the several well-authenticated cases he records under the heading "apparitions of the living," we feel assured that he will be convinced that man has a spiritual nature, which can exist either in or out of the body.

As the whole spiritualistic argument has been suspended upon this proposition, permit us to carry the argument further. The sin of prolixity is not so great as that of brevity, where there is so much at stake.

Of Mrs. Hauffe, the seeress of Prevorst, Kerner says, "She was more than half a spirit, and belonged to a world of spirits: she belonged to a world after death, and was more than half dead. In her sleep only was she truly awake. Nay, so loose was the connection between soul and body, that, like Swedenborg, she often went out of the body, and could contemplate it separately." — *Despair of Science*, p. 146.

The following, taken from "The Albany Times," seems to illustrate the truth of our proposition: —

"Some two weeks since, a young lady living here, whose father is engaged in mercantile business in this city, awoke from a sleep, feeling distressed and alarmed from the effects of an unpleasant dream. The gas-light was burning, but had been turned down to the closest point; thus making a dim light in the room, and rendering portions of it almost dark. Soon after awaking, the young lady's attention was attracted by the well-defined figure of a lady of her acquaintance moving from the door, some ten feet from the foot of her bed, toward it. Impulsively she called the figure by name, on the instant forgetting the improbability of the friend being in the house, and the fact that she was not a resident of the city, but resided in St. Louis. Soon, however, all this recurred to her, and the figure already neared the now alarmed girl. The form and features were perfect and distinct, the expression one of cheerful greeting; and, as it approached closer and closer to her side, it became dimmer and dimmer, and finally disappeared entirely when it had advanced to about half the length of the bed. The nervousness caused by this incident naturally enough induced the young lady to arouse the family, who ascribed the matter to exciting imaginings. But there was a singular sequel. She had forebodings, notwithstanding all that was said to calm them; and the next day wrote to her friend, detailing the incident. An answer was promptly received, announcing the good health of the writer, and the fact, that on the same night, and at the same hour, she had been visited in precisely the same manner by the semblance of her friend in Albany, and been alarmed thereby, lest it was the forerunner of evil. The mutual revelation was a relief to both. The circumstance, we think, has few, if any, parallels, and can partially be ascribed to the love the two girls had for each other, and to active nervous temperaments; but, as to an entirely satisfactory explanation of it, we think none can be given."

This circumstance is recorded as an historical fact, nothing more; and as such we demand that it be met. It will not do to laugh at these things; they won't be laughed down: they occur, and demand an explanation. Let the *savans* of science look at and explain a few such extracts as the foregoing; and, if that is not enough, here is another taken from "The Banner of Light:"—

"Question, by Hiram Dayton of Cincinnati, O.: I have always entertained strong doubts in regard to the real truth of spirit-communication; but a communication received by me on the night of Oct. 20 places me in a worse condition than ever. I believe, yea, I *know;* yet I do not believe, and *don't* know.

"On the night above referred to, I attended a small circle in the house of Mr. Brayton, on Ninth Street. The medium's name was Josephine Gray, whom I had never seen before; neither was I in the least acquainted with Mr. Brayton. When under the influence, my father came and spoke through her in a wonderfully mysterious manner.

"My father resides in Albany, N.Y., has lived there over forty years; yet he came and told me all about home, describing as correctly as I could have done; even giving names of persons, together with their streets and numbers, with whom I am acquainted; and, lastly, said he was very sick, and quite delirious, but thought he should recover soon.

"I could not gainsay the statement; but of his sickness I could not believe. The following day, I wrote him a letter, detailing all of the circumstances connected with the communication.

"On the 23d of October, I received a letter from my sister, stating that our father had been very sick, but was now better. But I heard nothing from my letter to him until the 12th of December, when I received a letter, written by his own hand, which states that on the 20th of October he was very sick, and says that my sister tells him he was quite delirious for two or three hours. My father says he has no recollection of what passed during the time referred to by my sister; neither does he remember of seeing or dreaming about me. He says, to him the two or three hours referred to were a perfect blank; and he does not appear to understand how he could converse through another without knowing it. Please explain this strange phenomenon."

With one more extract we will close this department of the subject.

"The Spiritual Telegraph" says, "A New-Haven gentleman relates the following: Some years ago, a gentleman of the name of Daboll, residing in New London, Conn., who was reputed to possess the faculty of seeing things in distant parts of the country, was applied to for information respecting a sea-captain and vessel which had sailed from that port, and concerning whose fate there was some uneasiness. The old gentleman retired, and shortly afterward returned, and said he had seen the captain at a certain porter-house at New Orleans, in the act of drinking a bowl of punch, and that he was then on the eve of sailing for home. The circumstance was noted down, together with the day and hour of the observation. In due time, the captain returned home with his vessel, and was questioned respecting his whereabouts on the day above referred to. He said, among other things, that he was at a certain porter-house in New Orleans, and that, as he was regaling himself with a bowl of punch, he plainly saw old Mr. Daboll come in at one door, and go out at another. Many of our readers will recollect an almost precisely similar circumstance related by Jung Stilling about an old seer who resided in solitude on the banks of the Delaware, near Philadelphia."

Such facts need no comment. When they are properly explained, the spiritual nature of man will appear. We ourself have had an experience somewhat similar to the one above related.

We have been so fortunate as to have had the privilege of conversing with several persons who had been supposed to be dead; some from drowning, some from wounds received in battle, and two or three who had been supposed to die a natural death, but had recovered from their catalepsy. In almost every instance, the subject has related an experience which proves him to have had a conscious existence separate from the physical organism. Some have told where they had been and what they had seen, and, occasionally, one has given an unmistakable test, by which we could know not only that the subject was sincere in thinking he had left his body, but that he had actually seen places and parties many miles away from his body, in some instances giving so many et cæteras, that he could not possibly have learned in any other way, that it would seem impossible to disbelieve his testimony.

We remember one individual in particular, who, being drowned and afterward resuscitated, in giving his experience, said, that while drowning, he *distinctly remembered every act of his life.* Matters of great and small importance were presented with like vivid distinctness; things long gone out of mind were as fresh to him as at the instant of their transaction. After viewing, as in panoramic scene, his own life, the vision faded before him. He then remembered leaving his body; of viewing himself in the water and out of the water at the same time; of being for a few moments confused to make out which was really himself, or whether it was not all a dream; of discovering a magnetic cord (could with propriety be termed a spiritual *umbilical* cord; Solomon calls it a "silver cord," Eccl. xii. 6) by which he was prevented from getting entirely away from the animal body, &c. The whole circumstance was related to us in such a serious manner, and with such an air of truthfulness, that we could come to no other conclusion than that to the relator it was a reality.

Now we are tempted to ask, What do such experiences mean? They are so many and so varied, that, if they were written, "the world itself could not contain the books." Yet not one who has ever passed through such a scene has had the hardihood afterward to deny his belief in his spiritual nature.

We now approach the second division of the argument, viz., —

The Spiritual Nature of Man exists in a Conscious State after the Body is dead.

Most Bible believers acknowledge this proposition. Some do not. For the benefit of such, we will state that it is a Bible doctrine, that knowledge inheres in spirit.

"For what man knoweth the things of a man, save the spirit of a man which is in him?" — 1 Cor. ii. 11.

This text affirms just what our proposition does, — that knowledge inheres in spirit. Paul once more makes the same affirmation. Hear him: —

"For we wrestle not against flesh and blood, but against principalities, against powers, against the rulers of the darkness of this world, against spiritual wickedness [wicked spirits] in high places." — Eph. vi. 12.

Certainly, wickedness can not be predicated of that which is not conscious; but it is predicated of spirit: *therefore* spirit is conscious.

No one will contend that the spirit who said to Philip, "Go near and join thyself to this chariot" (Acts viii. 29), was unconscious.

This same spirit gave a physical demonstration of his power when he "caught away Philip that the eunuch saw him no more." — Acts viii. 39.

The writer of the Book of Acts says, —

"For unclean spirits, crying with a loud voice, came out of many that were possessed with them; and many taken with palsies, and that were lame, were healed." — Acts viii. 7.

Permit us to ask, How could these unclean spirits take possession of media, and cry with a loud voice, if they had no conscious existence? Such paragraphs as the one just quoted can be found by the score in the Bible. Do they mean any thing? They do not, unless their writers supposed the spirit to be a conscious entity.

With the elucidation of one more thought, we will pass to the last and most important proposition of this chapter. Peter says, —

"For Christ also hath once suffered for our sins, the just for the unjust, that he might bring us to God; being put to death in the flesh, but quickened by the spirit: by which, also, he went and preached to the spirits in prison; which sometime were disobedient in the days of Noah, while the ark was preparing, wherein few, that is eight souls, were saved by water."—1 Pet. iii. 18–20.

In this text there are three expressions which should be weighed. 1st, "Christ being put to death in the flesh," i. e., the flesh being put to death, "but quickened by the spirit." The best scholars inform us that a better rendering would be, "Christ suffered the stroke of death in the flesh, but *survived it in the spirit.*" How plain! The flesh put to death, the spirit survives.

2d, The next point to which we would call attention is, "By which he [Christ, who survived in the spirit] went and preached to the spirits in prison."

3d, These spirits were departed spirits of human beings; for they were none other than those who were disobedient in the days of Noah. These spirits, certainly, could not hear preaching if they did not exist in a conscious state. This statement is corroborated by another statement from the same author.

"For this cause was the gospel preached also to them that are dead, that they might be judged according to men in the flesh, but live according to God in the spirit."—1 Pet. iv. 6.

What sense can there be in using the phrase, "men in the flesh," if there are no men out of the flesh,—if, indeed, flesh, blood, and breath is all there is of man?

We now come to a consideration of the argument from another standpoint. It is as follows: —

Spirits of the Departed can communicate with the Inhabitants of Earth.

This proposition is the "stumbling-block," this contains the offensive part, of Spiritualism; drop this, and a majority of our readers will admit the preceding ones. Only keep spirits away from this earth, keep heaven and earth apart, and all is well; but write that spirits in and out of the flesh hold sweet communion, and you are at once a heretic, worthy of nothing better than the fate of Michael Servetus, or the Salem witches.

On this, as on other departments of this subject, our first evidences shall be drawn from the Bible.

After having spent twelve years in the investigation of Spiritualism as an opponent, and almost six years as an advocate, we are compelled to say that modern Spiritualism is but a repetition of ancient Spiritualism, as manifest in the Bible. We can not now think of a form of manifestation in the Bible but that can be duplicated in modern manifestations, and *vice versâ.*

The case of Samuel returning to Saul is so irresistible, that we present it first. The historian prefaces his historical fact with the words, —

"Now, Samuel was dead, and all Israel had lamented him, and buried him in Ramah, even in his own city. And Saul had put away those that had familiar spirits, and the wizards, out of the land." — 1 Sam. xxviii. 3.

But the Jehovah being a "jealous God" (Ex. xx. 5) had become angry with Saul, and left him to manage his own affairs. In his extremity, Saul had recourse to other gods; for be it remembered, that while this Jewish God is nothing more nor less than the spirit of a dead man, as we will abundantly prove, every spirit that communicated was a god. Thus when a band of spirits, led on by Samuel the prophet, came to the woman, she said, "I saw gods ascending out of the earth." She immediately, in response to Saul's inquiry, proceeds to describe one. Her language is, "An old man cometh up, and he is covered with a mantle." From this description, Saul perceived that it was Samuel. Now, we will, without note or comment, let the historian tell his own story.

"And Samuel said to Saul, Why hast thou disquieted me, to bring me up? And Saul answered, I am sore distressed; for the Philistines make war against me, and God is departed from me, and answereth me no more, neither by prophets nor by dreams: therefore I have called thee, that thou mayest make known unto me what I shall do. Then said Samuel, Wherefore, then, dost thou ask of me, seeing the Lord is departed from thee, and is become thine enemy? And the Lord hath done to him as he spake by me; for the Lord hath rent the kingdom out of thine hand, and given it to thy neighbor, even to David. Because thou obeyedst not the voice of the Lord, nor executedst his fierce wrath upon Amalek, therefore hath the Lord done this thing unto thee this day. Moreover, the Lord will also deliver Israel with thee into the hand of the Philistines; and to-morrow shalt thou and thy sons be with me: the Lord, also, shall deliver the host of Israel into the hand of the Philistines. Then Saul fell straightway all along on the earth, and was sore afraid, because of the words of Samuel: and there was no strength in him; for he had eaten no bread all the day nor all the night."

We have given this whole history in order that our readers may see the similarity in ancient and modern Spiritualism. There is only one question underlying the whole circumstance; that is, *Is the Bible true?* If so, Samuel not only had a conscious existence after the world called him dead, but he returned to talk with Saul, who was an old acquaintance. If this record is not true, we ask the opponents of Spiritualism, in all candor, how they know that any of the Bible is true? The Bible says, "*Samuel said to Saul, Why hast thou disquieted me?*" &c. Christians, again we ask, Is your Bible true? If so, the question is settled.

"No," said a minister to us, "the Devil came to this old witch and Saul, personating Samuel." We could but ask, "Who told you so?"

But it matters not whether it was Samuel, the Devil, or an *ignis fatuus;* whether the woman was a witch, a medium, or a member of an orthodox Presbyterian church; to us and all others the evidence is the same. From it, in either case, the following stubborn conclusions are irresistible: —

1. It was the opinion of Saul (who was a Jewish prophet, and ought to know) that Samuel was there, and conversed with him.

2. The woman evidently thought Samuel was there.

3. The Jewish nation, "to whom were committed the oracles of God" (Rom. iii. 2) ever believed that Samuel was there.

4. The writer of the Book of Samuel says, without note or comment, Samuel was there. He makes no reservation, no explanation; records it, not as being a strange circumstance; but as a matter of course.

5. Finally, though we resisted the evidence twelve long years, we fully believe Samuel was there; we find no room to doubt it; as well doubt the fact of Saul or the woman having been present on that occasion.

Josephus, a Jewish historian, has said that the woman was a *necromancer;* that she saw Samuel. His account of the matter reads as follows: —

"She told Saul she saw an old man already, and of a glorious personage, and that he had on a sacerdotal mantle. So the king discovered by these signs that he was Samuel; and he fell down upon the ground, and saluted and worshiped him. And when the soul of Samuel asked him why he had disturbed him, and caused him to be brought up, he lamented the necessity he was under; for he said that his enemies pressed heavily upon him; that he was in distress what to do in his present circumstances; that he was forsaken of God, and could obtain no prediction of what was coming, neither by prophets nor by dreams; and that these are the reasons I have recourse to thee, who always takest care of me."

Upon this, one of our most pithy writers, W. F. Jamieson, remarks, "Poor, distressed Saul; my soul always sympathizes with him when I read the account. His guardian angel or spirit lord was thrown into a rage because Saul refused to obey him in the conduct of the war with the Amalekites. That Saul may have believed that the God of the universe was his adviser, and had refused to answer him because of his disobedience, is reasonable. There are people in this day who believe they talk with God. God is often belittled in the imagination as a fretful, passionate, finite being."

But Josephus continues, "But Samuel, seeing that the end of Saul's life was come, said, 'It is vain for thee to desire to learn of me any thing further, when God hath forsaken thee; however, hear what I say, that David is to be king, and to finish this war with good success; and thou art to lose thy dominion and thy life, because thou didst not obey God in the war with the Amalekites, and hast not kept his commandments as I foretold thee while I was alive.'" — *Antiquities of the Jews*, chap. xiv.

Since the opposers of modern Spiritualism are finding the conclusions Spiritualists draw from this irresistible, they have concluded to impede its force by slandering the character of the lady who officiated as medium on this occasion. In addition to calling her "an old witch," there has never been an insinuation made against the character of a modern medium but has been used to injure the reputation of the benevolent lady whom Saul sought in the hour of his distress. The object, of course, is to create a prejudice by which to kill the force of this manifestation. Happily, a Jewish historian has come to her rescue. The character of one medium, at least, finds a defender. Josephus says, —

"It is but just to recommend the generosity of this woman, because, when the king had forbidden her to use that art whence her circumstances were bettered and improved, and when she had never seen the king before, she still did not remember to his disadvantage that he had condemned her sort of learning, and did not refuse him as a stranger and one that she had no acquaintance with; but she had compassion upon him, and comforted him, and exhorted him to do what he was greatly averse to, and offered him the only creature she had, as a poor woman, and that earnestly and with great humanity, while she had no requital made her for her kindness, nor hunted after any future favor from him, for she knew that he was to die: whereas, men are naturally either ambitious to please those that bestow benefits upon them, or are very ready to serve those from whom they may receive some advantage. It would be well, therefore, to imitate the example of this woman, and do kindness to all such as are in want, and to think that nothing is better, nor more becoming mankind, than such general beneficence, nor what will sooner render God favorable, and ready to bestow good things upon us."

The case of the appearance of Moses and Elias is positive proof of our proposition. One writer records this phenomenon as follows: —

"And after six days Jesus taketh Peter, James, and John his brother, and bringeth them up into a high mountain apart, and was transfigured before them; and his face did shine as the sun, and his raiment was white as the light. And, behold, there appeared unto them Moses and Elias talking with him. Then answered Peter, and said unto Jesus, Lord, it is good for us to be here: if thou wilt, let us make here three tabernacles; one for thee, and one for Moses, and one for Elias. While he yet spake, behold, a bright cloud overshadowed them: and behold a voice out of the cloud, which said, This is my beloved Son, in whom I am well pleased: hear ye him. And, when the disciples heard it, they fell on their face, and were sore afraid. And Jesus came and touched them, and said, Arise, and be not afraid." — Matt. xvii. 1–7.

Luke's record is even more positive and spiritualistic than that of Matthew. As Luke has made some points worthy of attention, which Matthew did not mention, we quote his record entire: —

"And it came to pass about an eight days after these sayings, he took Peter and John and James, and went up into a mountain to pray. And as he prayed, the fashion of his countenance was altered, and his raiment was white and glistering. *And, behold, there talked with him two men, which were Moses and Elias,* who appeared in glory, and spake of his decease which he should accomplish at Jerusalem. But Peter and they that were with him were heavy with sleep; and, when they were awake, they saw his glory, and the two men that stood with him. And it came to pass, as they departed from him, Peter said unto Jesus, Master, it is good for us to be here: and let us make three tabernacles; one for thee, and one for Moses, and one for Elias; not knowing what he said. While he thus spake, there came a cloud and overshadowed them; and they feared as they entered into the cloud. And there came a voice out of the cloud, saying, This is my beloved Son: hear him. And when the voice was past, Jesus was found alone. And they kept it close, and told no man in those days any of those things which they had seen." — Luke ix. 28–36.

This can not be any thing else than the appearance of those we call dead; for the Bible says, —

"So Moses, the servant of the Lord, died there in the land of Moab, according to the word of the Lord. And he buried him in a valley in the land of Moab, over against Beth-peor; but no man knoweth of his sepulchre unto this day. And Moses was a hundred and twenty years old when he died: his eye was not dim, nor his natural force abated." — Deut. xxxiv. 5–7.

If the record is true, "there talked with him *two men, which were Moses and Elias.*" How can this be met? "Oh!" say our materialistic opposers, "it is only a vision: Moses and Elias were not there." We can not see how the declaration, "Tell the vision to no man," should lead us to dispute the record which says, "Moses and Elias talked with him," any more than the record which says, "They came, saying that they had also seen a vision of angels, which said that he was alive" (Luke xxiv. 23), should cause us to say that angels never come to earth. In this "vision," we have not only the talking of the dead to the living, but there was evidently a spirit-light; for Jesus is surrounded by a cloud so bright, that his face and garments are all aglow. The disciples were evidently unconsciously entranced; for Peter talked without knowing what he said. A spirit-voice, such as is now heard every day, was heard at this time, saying, "This is my beloved son."

We not only affirm that spirits can and do return and communicate, but that every form of the manifestation of modern Spiritualism is found in the Bible. Perhaps there is no form of mediumship now more popular than that of writing. There are now various phases of writing mediumship. Dr. Henry Slade of Jackson, Mich., and Peter West of Chicago, are, perhaps, the best writing mediums in the circle of our acquaintance. We have often known pencils to write in their presence, in broad daylight, without any visible hand touching them. There is a little girl not yet four years old, in Newton Corner, Mass., who has had the names of deceased persons come in large vivid letters upon her arm, when there was no visible cause for the strange manifestation. The "hand-writing" was never plainer on "the walls of the king's palace" than we ourself have seen it on the walls of our own bedroom. Some of the finest poems and plays we have ever read were written by an entranced medium.

Different phases of writing mediumship can be found in the Bible. After Elijah the prophet had been in the spirit-world at least seven years, we read, —

"And there came a writing to him [King Jehoram] from Elijah the prophet, saying, Thus saith the Lord God of David thy father, Because thou hast not walked in the ways of Jehoshaphat thy father, nor in the ways of Asa king of Judah, but hast walked in the way of the kings of Israel, and hast made Judah and the inhabitants of Jerusalem to go a whoring, like to the whoredoms of the house of Ahab, and also hast slain thy brethren of thy father's house, which were better than thyself, behold, with a great plague will the Lord smite thy people, and thy children, and thy wives, and all thy goods; and thou shalt have great sickness by disease of thy bowels, until thy bowels fall out by reason of the sickness day by day." — 2 Chron. xxi. 12–16.

This Jehoram was not exalted to the throne until

after Elisha's return from Elijah's funeral, when the two she bears killed the forty-two children (see 2 Kings ii. 23–25, iii. 1, 2); but this written communication from Elijah is the death-warrant of the king, whose wicked reign lasted eight years. Hence there is no escaping the fact that it is a genuine spirit-communication.

In Dan. v. 5, is another written communication. The words of the text are,—

"In the same hour came forth fingers of a man's hand, and wrote over against the candlestick upon the plaster of the wall of the king's palace; and the king saw the part of the hand that wrote."

Shall we believe such things in the Bible, and reject similar modern manifestations? Or, to reverse the proposition, are not modern phenomena a testimony to the truth of such declarations of holy writ?

We are not yet ready to take leave of the communications from and manifestations of the spirit of Elijah. The Jews had a tradition that Elias [Elijah the prophet] must come (Matt. xvii. 11). This tradition was, perhaps, based on the prediction,—

"Behold, I will send you Elijah the prophet before the coming of the great and dreadful day of the Lord." —Mal. iv. 5.

When the birth of John the Baptist was foretold, it was said of him,—

"And he shall go before him in the spirit and power of Elias, to turn the hearts of the fathers to the children, and the disobedient to the wisdom of the just; to make ready a people prepared for the Lord."—Luke i. 17.

John does go out in the spirit of Elijah, and manifests

all of his idiosyncrasies; and, as a result, the Jews exclaim, "He hath a Devil" (Matt. xi. 18). The word "devil," in this instance, comes from the Greek word *daimon*, which the Greeks, who should understand their own language, interpreted to mean the spirit of a dead man. How similar is this to the charge now brought against those under the influence of spirits!

To make assurance in regard to John being under Elijah's influence doubly sure, Jesus, after the martyrdom of John, says of him, "And, if ye will receive it, this is Elias which was for to come." — Matt. xi. 14. Again we read, —

"And his disciples asked him, saying, Why, then, say the scribes that Elias must first come? And Jesus answered and said unto them, Elias truly shall first come, and restore all things. But I say unto you, that Elias is come already, and they knew him not, but have done unto him whatsoever they listed. Likewise shall also the Son of man suffer of them. Then the disciples understood that he spake unto them of John the Baptist."

So far as argument from the Bible is concerned, we must consider the question settled. Though there are hundreds of passages in that book bearing upon the point, there are none more positive than many of those already quoted.

For the benefit of the curious who wish to pursue this part of the investigation further, we subjoin a few scriptural statements without comment. Ezekiel was a great medium, as will be evinced by the following: —

"Then the spirit took me up, and I heard behind me a voice of a great rushing, saying, Blessed be the glory of the Lord from his place." — Ezek. iii. 12.

"Then the spirit entered into me, and set me upon my feet, and spake with me, and said unto me, Go, shut thyself within thine house." — Ezek. iii. 24.

"Then I beheld, and, lo, a likeness as the appearance of fire; from the appearance of his loins, even downward, fire; and from his loins, even upward, as the appearance of brightness, as the color of amber. *And he put forth the form of a hand, and took me by a lock of mine head; and the spirit lifted me up between the earth and the heaven*, and brought me in the visions of God to Jerusalem, to the door of the inner gate that looketh toward the north; where was the seat of the image of jealousy, which provoketh to jealousy." — Ezek. viii. 2, 3.

Here is either a physical manifestation of spirit-power, or Ezekiel's spirit leaves his body, and is caught away "in the visions of God to Jerusalem." In either case, it affords the most positive proof of Spiritualism. The spirits with which Ezekiel deals to so great an extent are several times called men. — See Ezek. ix. 2, 3, 11.

"Afterwards the spirit took me up, and brought me in a vision by the Spirit of God into Chaldæa, to them of the captivity. So the vision that I had seen went up from me. Then I spake unto them of the captivity all the things that the Lord had showed me." — Ezek. xi. 24, 25.

Death did not change the moral status of men in ancient times more than it does now; hence, the spirits communicating were not always good and truthful. In 1 Sam. xvi. 14–17, we read, —

"But the spirit of the Lord departed from Saul, and an evil spirit from the Lord troubled him. And Saul's servants said unto him, Behold now, an evil spirit from God troubleth thee. Let our lord now command thy servants, which are before thee, to seek out a man who is a cunning player on a harp; and it shall come to pass when the evil spirit from God is upon thee, that he shall play with his hand, and thou shalt be well. And Saul said unto his servants, Provide me now a man that can play well, and bring him to me."

David was the man provided.

"And it came to pass, when the evil spirit from God was upon Saul, that David took a harp, and played with his hand: so Saul was refreshed, and was well, and the evil spirit departed from him." — 1 Sam. xvi. 23.

Lying spirits once got the control of four hundred prophets at one time. — See 1 Kings xxii.

Permit us, in conclusion, to present a few evidences from the pages of every-day life; and we must preface them with the truthful words of the renowned Dr. Johnson.

"That the dead are seen no more," says the great lexicographer, "I will not undertake to maintain against the concurrent testimony of all ages and nations. There is no people, rude or unlearned, among whom apparitions of the dead are not related and believed. This opinion, which prevails as far as human nature is diffused, could become universal only by its truth; those who never heard of one another would not have agreed in a tale which nothing but experience could make credible. That it is doubted by single cavilers can very little weaken the general evidence; and some who deny it with their tongues confess it with their fears."

Had our readers the time and disposition to candidly

peruse the works of Hon. Robert Dale Owen and William Howitt, on this subject, they would find a mine which would richly repay their explorations; besides, it would satisfy those who have brains, and use them, that the dead do return. The following extract, taken from "The Spiritual Times" of London, is to the point:—

"The Marquis de Bamtouillet and the Marquis de Precey were intimate friends and companions in arms. Talking, one day, of the next world, they promised that the one who died first should return to tell the other of the event. Three months subsequently, the Marquis de Bamtouillet started for the seat of war in Flanders: his friend, being detained by fever, remained in Paris. Six weeks later, De Precey was awakened at six o'clock in the morning by the curtains of his bed being drawn aside; and, turning to see who it was, he perceived his friend. Springing out of bed, he tried to embrace him, to testify his joy at his return; but Bamtouillet retreated a few steps, and said, caresses were misplaced; he came to fulfill a promise; that he had been slain in battle the preceding day, and that all that was said of a future life was true; that De Precey ought to alter his present mode of life without delay, for he would be killed in his first engagement. Unable to credit his senses, the marquis again tried to embrace his friend, believing it all to be a joke; but he only grasped the air: and Bamtouillet, perceiving his doubts, showed him the wound which he had received, from which the blood appeared to flow. After this, the phantom disappeared; and De Precey awoke the whole house by his cries. Several persons, to whom he related what he had seen and heard, attributed the vision to a fevered brain, and, entreating him to lie down, assured him that he must have been dreaming. The marquis, in despair at being taken for a visionary, related all the above-mentioned circumstances, protesting he had both seen and heard his friend while awake; but it was of no effect until the arrival of the mail from Flanders brought the announcement of the death of the marquis.

"This first circumstance proving correct, in the very manner related by De Precey, his friends began to think there might be some foundation for the adventure related; Bamtouillet having been killed on the eve of the day he announced the fact, and there not having elapsed time enough for the information to be received by natural means. The event was much canvassed in Paris, but attributed to a heated brain, in spite of the testimony of some who had examined the case seriously. The prediction was, however, shortly verified; for on the marquis's recovery, at the commencement of the civil wars, he proceeded at once to the scene of action, in spite of the urgent entreaties of his father and mother, who dreaded the fulfillment of the prophecy; and was killed at the battle of Saint Antoine."

The above we present as an historical fact. As such we demand that it be met. It is only one of a thousand. Philosophers and scientists, such facts demand your attention.

We will only add, the testimony concerning the *anastasis* of Jesus, which Peter calls *infallible*, is not half so good and well authenticated as testimony coming to earth's inhabitants every day, telling them of a "beyond," another side to the river of death, where those we mourn as lost wait with outstretched arms to receive us.

"It is a faith sublime and sure,
That ever round our head,
Are hovering on viewless wings
The spirits of the dead."

CHAPTER V.

THE BIRTH OF THE SPIRIT.

All Subjects Important—"Ye must be born again"—Nicodemus' Quandary—A Minister's Opinion—Author's Objection—Jesus' Tests—Must be born out of Flesh—Birth of the Spirit a Resurrection—Not of Flesh and Blood—Bible against it (1 Cor. xv.)—Natural and Spiritual Body—Opinion of the Woman of Tekoah—Of Job—Of Jesus—Objections answered—Mortal Bodies quickened—Must eat Christ's Flesh—Job and the Worms—Job refers to his Recovery—He did see God—Scientific Arguments—Change of Matter—Interesting Dialogue—Is the Mind an Entity—Abraham in the Resurrection—Dust returning to Dust—Resurrection a Birth—Jesus born of the Spirit—Seen by Clairvoyants—He goes and comes like the Wind—His Flesh and Bones—Owasso, the Boots and the Hand—His Explanation—Jesus appears to Paul—Others do not see him—Test from Ananias—Jesus, in showing himself, demonstrated Immortality—Practical Conclusions—Born into the Other World of this—Future Happiness and Misery made by Life here—Alexander Campbell—The Good shall shine—Spirits and Tobacco—Appetites may be our Hell hereafter—Admonition.

THOUGH very popular, it is hardly just to say of any question, "This is important," as such language implies that there are questions of no importance; which is not the case. Every truth has its bearing on every other truth; every truth received is a light by which we may be enabled to discover kindred truths; every truth rejected is a light extinguished; and darkness is the result.

"Ye must be born again," is the language of Jesus to Nicodemus: and every one who believes his Bible indorses it; the only question being, What is meant by being born again? There is a difference, "wide as the world," between our views and those of our Christian neighbors, as to what constitutes the birth of the spirit.

Jesus, in his conference with a member of the Jewish senate, said, "Except a man be born again, he can not see the kingdom of God." This astonished Nicodemus, who could not see how it would be possible for him, under the circumstances, to get into the kingdom; for he was already an old man: and how could an old man be born? Jesus answers,—

"Verily, verily, I say unto thee, Except a man be born of water and of the Spirit, he can not enter into the kingdom of God. That which is born of the flesh is flesh; and that which is born of the Spirit is spirit. Marvel not that I said unto thee, Ye must be born again."—John iii. 5–7.

Sawyer renders this, "That which is born of the Spirit is a spirit."

Here the matter is explained. It is the birth of the Spirit that Jesus is speaking of, as much as to say, "You got your fleshly existence, got into this fleshly kingdom, by a birth of the flesh; now, in order to enter upon your spiritual existence, that is, your existence where there is no flesh and blood, you must be born of the Spirit. Don't wonder that I told you you must be born again."

"The wind bloweth where it listeth, and thou hearest the sound thereof, but canst not tell whence it cometh, and whither it goeth: so is every one that is born of the Spirit."—John iii. 8.

When but a boy, we once asked a minister for an explanation of this verse. He kindly consented to give us the needed light. "The birth of the Spirit," said he, "is nothing more nor less than conversion. All who are converted are born again. The Spirit is like the wind ; it comes and goes, and you can not tell whence it comes, or whither it goes. You can not see the wind; you see its effects, and feel it: so you can not see the Spirit; but you do see and feel its operations on the heart."

This is substantially the theory of the orthodox world: it may do as a hypothesis; but it will not do as an explanation of this text. The text does not say, "The Spirit comes and goes like the wind," as this theory would have it, but "The wind bloweth where it listeth [pleaseth], and you can not tell where it comes from, or whither it goes: *so is every one that is born of the Spirit.*" Thus it is the individual born of the Spirit who goes and comes, *and you can not tell where he goes to or comes from.* Is it so with churchmen? Can they go and come without being detected, more than sinners, who never belonged to a church? They can not. Then we must decide that they have not experienced the birth spoken of in this text.

We do not deny that Christians may have experienced a change: no doubt they have; but we do deny that they have been born again. Jesus gives another *test* by which to try those professing to be born of the Spirit. "That which is born of the flesh is flesh, and that which is born of the Spirit is spirit" (is a spirit. — *Sawyer*). Are not churchmen flesh and blood in the same sense as sinners who do not belong to the church? But those born of the Spirit *are no longer flesh.*

"Except a man be born again, he can not see the kingdom of God." We might ask, Why? Paul answers, —

"Now, this I say, brethren, that flesh and blood can not inherit the kingdom of God; neither doth corruption inherit incorruption."—1 Cor. xv. 50.

This whole chapter is an argument showing the necessity of a resurrection in order to get into the kingdom of God, as Jesus shows the necessity of a spiritual birth in order to get into the kingdom. The verse above quoted tells why a resurrection is necessary: it is because "*flesh and blood can not inherit the kingdom.*" A resurrection, then, delivers us from flesh and blood: the birth of the Spirit does the same. For this and other reasons, we claim that the birth of the Spirit is the resurrection from the dead.

Here, before arguing this point, we must tell what we mean by the term "resurrection." We do not, by this term, mean, as many others do, the re-collecting of the particles of matter, and converting them once more into flesh, blood, and bone, and making them live again. That can not be done, as we will show. By the term "resurrection," we mean just what the Greeks meant by the term *anastasis*,—an elevation. Sometimes they used the term *ex-anastasis*. This will be found in Phil. iii. 11, where Paul says, "If by any means I might attain unto the resurrection of the dead." The Greek is, *ex-anastasin ton nekron*, which literally signifies, "resurrection out of the dead." How plain! The body dies, and man is born out of it. This is the resurrection.

Before attempting to prove that the birth of the Spirit and resurrection of the dead are the same, we will show that the body never will be raised to life.

No one contends that there are any scientific arguments for the resuscitation of the flesh. All science is confessedly against it: yet some say, "The Bible says so; and, though we can not comprehend it, we believe God has power to bring it about." Now, we emphatically deny that the Bible, when rightly interpreted, teaches any such doctrine: on the other hand, it is squarely against it.

The text above quoted is pointed and emphatic. If the kingdom of God is the state to be obtained at the resurrection, and "flesh and blood can not inherit the kingdom," then, whatever inference may be drawn from Paul's argument in other places, he has here positively committed himself as an unbeliever in the resurrection of the flesh. This whole chapter is worthy of attention: it is all devoted to this resurrection question. Any one who will read this chapter with the idea that Paul is arguing with Epicureans, who did not believe in any future life for man, will discover that he was simply arguing an existence for man beyond this mundane life, and not urging any particular form of resurrection, or definition of the term *anastasis*.

Paul bases the whole argument on certain phenomena, which he, and about five hundred others, had witnessed. Christ, he argued, had been seen after his assassination; therefore he was not dead. Christ lived after he was killed; therefore others would live after the event called death. He urges that there is life for man, as evinced by Christ being seen alive after his death, unless the witnesses who testified to having seen him were false; but he was seen on so many occasions, and by so many, that it could not have been falsehood or deception. He urges, further, that the witnesses were honest, as was proved by their jeopardizing their lives for their testimony. In 1 Cor. xv. 32, he says, —

"If, after the manner of men, I have fought with beasts at Ephesus, what advantageth it me, if the dead rise not? let us eat and drink; for to-morrow we die."

Thus he stakes his life on his hope of a resurrection, and, at the same time, informs his brethren that flesh and blood can not be raised.

When certain ones ask, "How are the dead raised up? and with what body do they come?" he answers, "Thou sowest not that body that shall be, but bare grain, it may chance of wheat, or of some other grain; but God giveth it a body as it hath pleased him, and to every seed his own body." — Verses 37, 38.

Every seed sown has God's own body. He continues urging that all bodies are not *earthly;* that there are *celestial* as well as *terrestrial* bodies, and, finally, says, —

"It is sown a natural body, it is raised a spiritual body. There is a natural body, and there is a spiritual body." — Verse 44.

All agree that a better rendering would be, "It is sown an *animal* body, it is raised a *spiritual* body. *There is an animal body, and there is a spiritual body.*" Now we inhabit an *animal* body; when born of the Spirit, we shall inhabit the *spiritual* body. Then will we have dropped "this mortal flesh," and been born into the higher life, called, in this text, "the kingdom of God."

Lest some should continue, notwithstanding the positive Scriptures we have quoted, to think that the flesh is to be raised from the dead, we will quote a few paragraphs from the "Book of books," which are so emphatic, that their meaning can not be questioned.

The wise woman of Tekoah, who went to David to make a plea in behalf of his rebellious son, in the course of her argument, said, —

"For we must needs die, and are as water spilt on the ground, which can not be gathered up again; neither doth God respect any person; yet doth he devise means, that his banished be not expelled from him." — 2 Sam. xiv. 14.

In a proper place we shall examine this from the philosopher's point of view. Then we shall show that this is literally true. That which goes to the ground *can not be gathered up again.*

Job, when he thought himself on his death-bed, said, —

"As the cloud is consumed, and vanisheth away, so he that goeth down to the grave shall come up no more. He shall return no more to his house, neither shall his place know him any more." — Job vii. 9, 10.

Stronger language could not be used. How persons can pretend to believe the Bible, and yet argue a resuscitation of the flesh, in the face of such positive declarations, we can not conceive. Comments on such paragraphs would be like holding up a rushlight, by which to view the shining sun.

Again: this same poet has said, —

"But man dieth and wasteth away: yea, man giveth up the ghost, and where is he? As the waters fail from the sea, and the flood decayeth and dryeth up, so man lieth down and riseth not: till the heavens be no more, they shall not awake, nor be raised out of their sleep." — Job xiv. 10–12.

Until the heavens be no more is the longest time he

could fix. If this text is true, man never can come out of the grave; for the graves where men sleep are all in the earth: but, when the heavens pass away, earth with all its graves passes too. John says, —

"And I saw a new heaven and a new earth; for the first heaven and the first earth were passed away: and there was no more sea." — Rev. xxi. 1.

Again: he says, "And I saw a great white throne, and him that sat on it, from whose face the earth and the heaven fled away; and there was found no place for them." — Rev. xx. 11.

Now, we submit, that if heaven, and earth with all its cemeteries filled with dead bodies, is gone so that *it can not be found*, and the dead are not raised out of the earth until after that time, as Job asserts, the chance for the resurrection of dead bodies is so small, that we do not wonder that Watts said, —

> "Great God, on what a slender thread
> Hang all eternal things!"

Jesus, in his conversation with the Sadducees, proves the doctrine of the resurrection by the fact that God was said to be the God of Abraham, Isaac, and Jacob, after they had been dead several hundred years. "But," said he, "God is not the God of the dead, but of the living:" so all these patriarchs are alive. His words are, —

"Now that the *dead are raised*, even Moses showed at the bush, when he calleth the Lord the God of Abraham, and the God of Isaac, and the God of Jacob; for he is not a God of the dead, but of the living; for all live unto him." — Luke xx. 37, 38.

Now, in all candid honesty, permit us to ask our readers, Do you believe that *the dead are raised*, as Jesus asserted, and was proved to Moses by the angel in the bush? or do you look forward to a time in the distant future when the dead *shall* be raised? We assert, without fear of successful contradiction, that the doctrine of a physical resurrection is *made for and not by the Bible.*

As the positions of our opposers on this subject can not well come under the head of objections, we will proceed to an explanation of such biblical expressions as are supposed to teach the resurrection of the body.

Perhaps nothing in the Bible is relied on to prove the resurrection of the flesh more than the following: "But, if the Spirit of Him that raised up Jesus from the dead dwell in you, he that raised up Christ from the dead shall also quicken your mortal bodies by his *Spirit* that dwelleth in you." — Rom. viii. 11.

This text says not one word about the *re*making and *re*vivifying of *dead* bodies. It only speaks of the *quickening of mortal bodies.* There is a vast difference between a mortal body and a dead body. Our mortal body has been quickened a number of times, and that by a spirit-power; but there never was a dead body raised to life. It would seem that the theory of a resurrection of the animal body must be hard pressed for evidence when it grasps at such "straws:" truly, it reminds us of the proverb concerning "drowning men."

"You speak," said an opponent in debate with us, "against the resurrection of the flesh. Job says, his flesh shall be raised from the dead: I believe in taking the Bible as it reads."

"Very well," said we, "let us take a paragraph literally. Jesus says, —

"'I am the living bread which came down from heaven. If any man eat of this bread, he shall live for ever; and the bread that I will give is my flesh, which I will give for the life of the world. The Jews, therefore, strove among themselves, saying, How can this man give us his flesh to eat? Then Jesus said unto them, Verily, verily, I say unto you, Except ye eat the flesh of the Son of man, and drink his blood, ye have no life in you. Whoso eateth my flesh and drinketh my blood hath eternal life; and I will raise him up at the last day. For my flesh is meat indeed, and my blood is drink indeed. He that eateth my flesh and drinketh my blood dwelleth in me, and I in him. As the living Father hath sent me, and I live by the Father, so he that eateth me, even he shall live by me. This is that bread which came down from heaven: not as your fathers did eat manna, and are dead. He that eateth of this bread shall live for ever.'" — John vi. 51–58.

Shall we all turn cannibals because Jesus said, "Except ye eat the flesh of the Son of man, and drink his blood, ye have no life in you"? It is, according to a strictly literal rendering of this passage, our only chance for salvation. If those who believe in a fleshly resurrection could find as positive a declaration that the flesh should come out of the grave, as this, that Christians must eat the flesh and drink the blood of Jesus, with what eagerness would they grasp it! Do, Christians, in heaven's name, be consistent! Now, we deny that Job or any other Bible writer said that his flesh should come out of the grave: on the other hand, we have shown that he said just the opposite.

Here is the text supposed to teach a physical anastasis.

"Oh that my words were now written! oh that they were printed in a book! that they were graven with an iron pen and lead in the rock for ever! for I know that my Redeemer liveth, and that he shall stand at the latter day upon the earth. And though after my skin worms destroy this body, yet in my flesh shall I see God, whom I shall see for myself, and mine eyes shall behold, and not another, though my reins be consumed within me." — Job xix. 23–27.

If this text teaches a material resurrection, Job squarely disputes in it what he said in chapters vii., xiv., and xvi. This we can not accuse Job of doing. This text has no more reference to the future of this life than though there was no future for man. Let it be remembered that Job was greatly afflicted at this time; his friends had forsaken him, he was covered with sore boils from the crown of his head to the sole of his feet (see Job ii. 7); that his wife advised him to curse God and die (Job ii. 9). This disease was caused by an animalculo preying upon his flesh: so that Job says, "My flesh is clothed with worms and clods of dust; my skin is broken, and become loathsome." — Job vii. 5.

In this very speech, he states that his friends, wife, servants, and all, had forsaken him: though he entreated his wife for his children's sake, yet she turned against him. His bone cleaved to his skin, and he escaped with the skin of his teeth. He then breaks out in the language just quoted, expressing his confidence that he will recover, though worms were consuming his flesh. Job did recover, and became a hearty old man.

"Ah, but Job said, 'In my flesh shall I see God.' Did he see God?" We answer most emphatically, "He did." The ancients saw God in bodily health and its attendant blessings. God was anciently in every gentle breeze, in the warm sunshine, the genial shower; in fact, in every pleasant sensation. When God withdrew his face, then the storm, the blight, the mildew, and pestilence raged; then it was that disease preyed upon its victims. By and by the face of God was again seen; and peace, happiness, and prosperity was the result.

Reader, this is not imagination: we are not left to guess on this point. After Job's recovery, God answers him in such a way, that Job is convinced that he is holding converse with the Infinite. Then Job says, —

"I have heard of thee by the hearing of the ear; but now mine eye seeth thee. Wherefore I abhor myself, and repent in dust and ashes." — Job xlii. 5, 6.

Thus every part of the text was fulfilled without a resurrection.

Now, having shown that the doctrine of a physical resurrection is not a Bible doctrine, we propose to take it from modern theologians, by showing that it is an impossibility, and therefore could not be true, even if it were taught in the Bible.

It is now an almost universally conceded fact that the entire matter of the human frame changes as often as once in seven years. Not long since, however, it was our fortune to hold a public discussion with a minister, who pretended to some knowledge of science, who denied this fact, and, to prove himself correct in his denial, triumphantly stripped up his sleeve to show a scar on his arm that he had carried nearly forty years.

"There," said this oracle of antiquated theology, "why did not that scar go when matter was passing off?" He might as well have asked why his eye or ear did not pass off with other matter. This reminds us that we once made the assertion that there is no *inertia:* every particle of steel in the razor-blade revolves around its fellow particle with all the precision that planets move in their courses. "Why," said an astonished opponent, "that is self-evidently false. I put my razor away, and always find it where I left it, which could not be the case if it were moving all the time." The poor man could not see the difference between particles revolving around each other, and razors moving off in bulk. So with this minister and his scar: the truth is, the scar had passed off several times within the period named, but each particle had retained its place until crowded out by another just like it; so that the size and shape of the scar was not changed in the operation more than a pyramid of apples would change by a purchaser buying an apple from the pyramid, and the grocer dropping another in its place.

For the benefit of Adventists, and all others who can not see any thing of man but flesh and blood, we will review this position at length.

Imagine the following dialogue between an elder of the materialistic school, who can see no future for man other than by a physical resurrection, and a philosopher, whose researches prevent his acceptance of that theory.

ELDER. — "Man is to be raised out of the ground, 'and the sea shall give up the dead which are in it.'"

PHILOSOPHER. — "How can that be, since matter is continually changing, and man does not, any one year of his life, possess the same body he had any previous year? Beside, is not the spirit or mind the real man? what need of a remolding and bringing to life of the flesh?"

Eld. — "Ah, friend! you err in two points. First, let me inform you that mind is not an entity, as you suppose, it is only a function of the brain. Brain grinds out thought. Mind is the result of the organization, and proper combination with the atmosphere, of the machinery called man, as the keeping of time is the result of the organization and setting in motion of the machine called the watch. Second, that matter does not change as you suppose, I will prove by a scar that I have carried more than forty years."

Phil. — "As to your first position, it is either true or false. If true, your second argument is not needed. If false, your second argument will only fall of its own weight. If the identity of man is not preserved, there can be no resurrection; possibly there could be a new creation. God could make a man out of every stone in the 'Granite State;' but he can not make Abraham or Moses out of these stones, from the fact that identity consists, in part at least, of the memory of past events; and those men made of stones could not recognize themselves as being the Abraham and Moses of old. Neither could the particles of matter which constituted the physical of Abraham and Moses at any one time be the same Abraham and Moses, for the reason that *the mind* of these men was the result of their organization, and, being dependent on the organism, could not exist after the physical man was disorganized."

Eld. — "Let me interrupt you: you are partly correct, and partly incorrect. The mind ceases to exist when the brain, its fountain, ceases to act; but when the brain is *re*-organized, of course the mind, which is a result, begins to act as before."

PHIL. — "Not so fast. The old mind was the result of the old organism, and, per consequence, ceased to exist when the old brain ceased its action. The *new mind* is the result not of the old *but of the new organism;* is ground out by the new brain, and, being the effect or function of the *new brain*, — made, for aught I care, of the old material, — can not antedate its existence. *Memory*, being a function of the mind, can not go back of the mind out of which it proceeds; but that mind was the result of the new organism: hence, the man before death can not possibly be connected with the man after the resurrection."

ELD. — "There are difficulties; but God has power, and 'these dry bones shall live.' The identity is not preserved in the mind, as that ceases to exist, but in the particles of matter of which the body is composed."

PHIL. — "Then you have lost your identity even while you live, and at this moment are losing part of it; for you are trimming your finger-nails. These nails are a part of the essential elder with whom I am talking, and, if the particles are all to be raised, must come up in the general resurrection, and be joined to your fingers, lest you should lose your identity. Your hair, which was once short enough, got too long, and you had it trimmed last week. Did you know the hair taken off your head once went into your stomach as food, then went frolicking and frisking through your veins, and from that time forward was a part of your essential identity, and as such claims a part in the resurrection.

body? Again: in your tedious spell of typhoid fever last winter, you lost twenty-five pounds of flesh. Where did that flesh go? It, too, claims a part in the resurrection-body. Notwithstanding your friends supposed you would die, you recovered; that is, all except the twenty-five pounds of you which died and left you. As soon as you became convalescent, your appetite began to return, you ate more heartily than before, and, as a result, found yourself increasing in weight at the rate of a pound a day, until you weighed more than before your sickness. Where did this second twenty-five pounds of flesh come from? Where was it while you were wearing the flesh you lost during your sickness? Let me tell you. Part of it was in the apple-orchard, in the shape of unripe fruit. Some of it was in the garden and potato patch; some swimming in the ocean, in the shape of codfish and mackerel; some of it growing in the coffee and tea fields; other portions were in the air, the water, &c. Now, your present flesh is as much a part of you as that you lost, and *vice versâ*. Which will you have raised from the dead, — the first, or the second? One has died, the other will die. Will you have both raised? Then, why not have all the matter that ever formed a part of your body brought back to it? Abraham lived a hundred and seventy-five years: that was long enough to wear out *twenty-five* bodies. Which one of these bodies shall be brought up from the grave? Or shall all of them come up? If so, there will be 'giants in those days.' *Abraham will have a beard forty feet long, and can not weigh less than two tons.*"

ELD. — "You ask questions faster than I can answer

them. Some questions can not be answered. We receive certain statements because God made them, not because we can answer every question concerning them. You ask, Which one of Abraham's bodies will come to life? We have an example furnished us in the resurrection of our Saviour. The same body that died was the one raised: so it will be in the case of Abraham."

Phil. — "But Abraham's twenty-five bodies each died, one no more than another. Not a particle of matter passed from either body till the body had used up all the life it could appropriate, and its very death sent it from the body to feed the life of vegetation; and, as it was resurrected in vegetation, it was eaten by animals and men, and, in turn, took its place in other bodies, *ad infinitum*. If you present the case of Jesus as an *example* to prove that the last body that dies, or the one that dies all at once, is the one to be raised, you are unfortunate: for the case selected proves the contrary. If Jesus' body that was killed came up from the grave, that, instead of proving that others will have a similar experience, proves directly the contrary. Jesus' body was made of what he ate, drank, and breathed; but the corn that he and his disciples plucked and ate on the sabbath day, as well as all other food that ever went into his stomach, had been fattened on the dead: it drew its life from the decomposition of animal and vegetable bodies. Thus all of Jesus' body was made by the death of other bodies; but his body, according to your theory, was brought up out of the tomb, revivified, and taken to heaven.

"Now think of the general resurrection, when millions upon millions of bodies shall be called from their beds of dust. Among them are the martyrs, whose bodies were burned to ashes, and the ashes scattered to the four winds by their persecutors, to prevent their resurrection: thus their ashes have fattened the soil of earth, as our southern battle-fields were fattened by the flesh, blood, and bones of poor soldiers. This soil has produced vegetation, which has been eaten by the 'cattle upon a thousand hills.' The cattle, made fat upon that which was once flesh of our flesh and bone of our bone, have, in their turn, been slain and eaten up to supply other bodies with aliment. The fluids of these bodies whose solids have thus been scattered have a thousand times arisen in the atmosphere, and a thousand times been condensed, and fallen in 'gentle dew and summer showers,' only to be evaporated to again fall to water the earth, wash the shores of the Atlantic, or be drunk by man and beast: thus these particles of matter, after having existed in ten thousand forms, and, for aught we can know to the contrary, in a thousand bodies, at the moment of death must be raised from the dead, when, to say the least, Jesus had taken part of them and gone to heaven!"

ELD.—"I must go. Good-day."

PHIL.—"Don't go yet; I find some figures here made to my hand, which I wish you to hear me read:—

"'DUST RETURNING TO DUST.—It is asserted by scientific writers that the number of persons who have existed on our globe since the beginning of time amounts to 36,627,843,273,075,256. These figures, when divided by 3,095,000 (the number of square leagues on the globe), give 11,320,689,732 square miles of land; which, being divided as before, give 1,314,622,076 persons to each square mile. If we reduce these miles to square rods, the number will be 1,853,174,600,000; which, divided in like manner, will give 1,283 inhabitants to each square rod, and these, being reduced to feet, will give about five persons to each square foot of *terra firma.* It will thus be perceived that our earth is a vast cemetery. On each square rod of it, 1,283 human beings lie buried; each rod being scarcely sufficient for ten graves, with each grave containing 128 persons. The whole surface of the earth, therefore, has been dug over 128 times to bury its dead.' From this extract, it will be seen that there is not dust enough now, if all the soil were converted to dust, to remake all the bodies that have existed on earth."

ELD. — "These difficulties are not for me to settle: I only receive the Bible. If you hope to find a theological system with no difficulties in its way, all I have to say is, you are having a bootless search. Good-day."

Yes: the elder thinks *he* has the Bible; and, like thousands of others who never had a liberal thought, it is all he asks. Those who have read this book thus far, can, perhaps, decide whether it is the Bible, or merely his *ipse dixit,* that teaches his peculiar views of the resurrection.

Now, having shown from the Bible and science, that the *anastasis* must be a *spiritual,* and not a physical event, we will pass to our main proposition, viz., that the spiritual birth is the resurrection.

The resurrection is several times said to be a birth. Paul says of Jesus Christ, —

"And he is the head of the body, the church; who is the beginning, the first-born from the dead, that in all things he might have the pre-eminence. For it pleased the Father that in him should all fullness dwell." — Col. i. 18, 19.

In Rev. i. 5, John says, —

"And from Jesus Christ, who is the faithful witness, and the first-begotten of the dead, and the prince of the kings of the earth. Unto him that loved us, and washed us from our sins in his own blood."

The word rendered *first-begotten* and *first-born* are the same; thus we have the Bible twice asserting that Jesus was born from death. "But," says the objector, "Jesus was the *first*-born from the dead: how can that be, if every one who had died before him had experienced this resurrection?" We answer, "There are two senses in which the word 'first' is used; sometimes it signifies the first in numerical order, and sometimes first in rank or importance, as, for instance, 'The lieutenant-general is the first military officer in the United States.' 'The office of President is the first office in the power of the American people to bestow.' The word rendered *first-born* and *first-begotten* in these two instances is the Greek word *prototokos*, which Greenfield defines to be, 'chief,' 'principal,' 'beloved,' &c."

The idea of the text is not that Jesus was the first one born from the dead, but that he is chief among those who have experienced this birth. Paul gives as a reason why he was the first-born, "that in all things he might have the pre-eminence. For it pleased the Father that in him should all fullness dwell." John uses the term to signify that he is "prince of the kings of the earth." As Jesus stood in the front ranks of reformers in this life, as he led their van, so, on the other side, in the kingdom to which he is now born, he occupies the front position. In this sense, and this alone, he is *first* among those born from the dead.

Jesus gives two tests by which to try those born of the Spirit.

1st, "That which is born of the flesh is flesh, and that which is born of the Spirit is spirit."

2d, "They who are born of the Spirit, like the wind go and come, and you can not tell where they go, or whence they come."

Now, let us apply these rules to Jesus after his resurrection. The various appearances of Jesus are enough to convince the candid reader that he did not bring his flesh up from the grave. Had his flesh been made alive, he could have been seen by the whole Jewish nation; and thus they could have been convinced of life and immortality. But he was not seen by all. Peter says, —

"Him God raised up the third day, and showed him openly; *not to all the people, but unto witnesses chosen before of God,* even to us, who did eat and drink with him after he rose from the dead." — Acts x. 40, 41.

How could Jesus have escaped being seen by the multitude, had he been flesh and blood, especially if he was openly among them? "Chosen witnesses" alone, who evidently were clairvoyant, had the privilege of seeing him. Mark says, —

"After that he appeared in another form unto two of them, as they walked, and went into the country." — Mark xvi. 12.

Physical bodies do not change their form in such a way as this text represents; but clairvoyants of every age of the world testify that spirits do assume different garbs and forms to suit the occasion.

Permit us now to devote a few words to Jesus' second test. Does he, after his birth from death, come and go in such a manner that it can not be told whence he comes and whither he goes? He does. Luke says, —

"And, behold, two of them went that same day to a village called Emmaus, which was from Jerusalem about threescore furlongs. And they talked together of all these things which had happened. And it came to pass, that, while they communed together and reasoned, Jesus himself drew near, and went with them. But their eyes were holden that they should not know him. And he said unto them, What manner of communications are these that ye have one to another, as ye walk, and are sad?" — Luke xxiv. 13–17.

Where did Jesus come from? The first his disciples knew, he was journeying with them, talking with them, "reasoning out of the law of Moses and the prophets." "But their eyes were holden that they should not know him." The "holding" of their eyes consisted in his appearing in a form that they could not recognize, as stated in Mark xvi. 12.

Those born of the Spirit are not only to come in this mysterious manner, but they are to go quite as unaccountably. Luke, in this same narrative, proceeds: —

"And they drew nigh unto the village whither they went; and he made as though he would have gone further. But they constrained him, saying, Abide with us for it is toward evening, and the day is far spent. And he went in to tarry with them And it came to pass, as he sat at meat with them, he took bread, and blessed it, and brake, and gave to them. And their eyes were opened, and they knew him; and he vanished out of their sight." — Mark xvi. 28–32.

Here Jesus has *vanished* or *faded* out of their sight, as spirits vanish from the sight of media every day. Now he has gone, and they could not tell whither he went. Has he in this proved himself born of the Spirit? But Luke proceeds: —

"And they said one to another, Did not our heart burn within us while he talked with us by the way, and while he opened to us the Scriptures? And they rose up the same hour, and returned to Jerusalem, and found the eleven gathered together, and them that were with them, saying, The Lord is risen indeed, and hath appeared to Simon. And they told what things were done in the way, and how he was known of them in breaking of bread. And, as they thus spake, Jesus himself stood in the midst of them, and saith unto them, Peace be unto you. But they were terrified and affrighted, and supposed that they had seen a spirit. And he said unto them, Why are ye troubled? and why do thoughts arise in your hearts? Behold my hands and my feet, that it is I myself. Handle me and see; for a spirit hath not flesh and bones as ye see me have. And, when he had thus spoken, he showed them his hands and his feet. And while they yet believed not for joy, and wondered, he said unto them, Have ye here any meat? And they gave him a piece of a broiled fish, and of a honeycomb. And he took it, and did eat before them." — Mark xvi. 32–43.

One point in this, that of fastening the doors, we will leave John to bring to light. It is enough for us at present to know, that, when they first saw Jesus, they only saw dim, shadowy outlines; for it is not until Jesus calls attention to his hands and feet, that they saw them.

"Ah," said Elder G——, "you have the wrong text here; for he *was not a spirit*, as his disciples supposed, and as you suppose; *but he had flesh and bones:* so the text is positive proof of the physical resurrection."

Not so fast. If the rendering of the text is correct, the disciples supposed they had seen a spirit, which is positive proof that they believed not only in the existence of spirits, but that they could return, and make themselves manifest. So far, we will set the text down as a positive proof of Spiritualism.

Now for a few words of criticism. If the reader will turn to the margin of Greenfield's Greek Testament, or to Griesbach's Greek Testament, he will find the word rendered "spirit," in this instance, is not the word *pneuma*, which is rendered "spirit" more than a hundred times in the New Testament, but *phantasma*, which is defined to be a phantom; that is, an appearance, something not real, some such spirit as the drunkard sees when he has the delirium tremens. With this interpretation, which no scholar will dispute, Jesus does not deny being a spirit: he only denies being a *phantom*, "the stuff that dreams are made of." "But he claims to have flesh and bones, so he must have had a physical body." No, dear reader: you have not read that correctly. He does not claim to have flesh and bones, but claims to *appear* to have them. The text does not say, "A spirit has not flesh and bones as I have," but "as *ye see me have*." The word rendered "see" in this instance is *theosia*, a word which signifies an appearance, and not a reality. The idea of the text is, that the flesh and bones were not a *reality*, but *an appearance* for the occasion. Do you ask how this can be? We frankly acknowledge we can not tell: we only know, from this text and from experience, that it is so.

It has been our good fortune to travel some with Dr. Henry Slade, an individual whom we can recommend anywhere as being a medium through whom satisfactory evidence of immortality can be given to any honest inquirer. Early in the month of October, 1864, we staid all night with the doctor at the Waverley House in Rochester, N.Y. The moon was shining brilliantly; and the windows and blinds, in consequence of the excessively warm evening, were opened. Not long after we had been in bed, the manifestations, as usual, commenced. Soon we saw our boots walking about the room with no visible feet or legs in them. We at once addressed the power thus propelling things about the room, and said, —

"I have seen your manifestations often. I know you exist, I know you have power; but why do you never let me see you? I want to see the power by which these wonderful things are done."

The intelligent power to whom we addressed this language said, "I will try. If conditions are such that I can gather a body from the elements, I will let you see me." We waited long and patiently for the promised manifestation. By and by, however, we heard a strange sound, and looked in the direction whence it proceeded, and saw a hand and arm coming toward us. We raised up in bed, reached out our hand and took hold of the hand, grasped it with a firm grip, determined to hold on, and, if possible, keep it as a trophy. It was to all appearance flesh and bone; at least we would have sworn it to be just such a hand as our own, only very much darker, and at least one-third longer. Soon we discovered that the arm began to grow shorter. As we saw it vanishing, as Jesus did from his disciples, we grasped the fingers more firmly; but, notwithstanding our determination, the arm, then the hand, then the fingers, dissolved, leaving us to grasp the air.

In a moment, the Indian was laughing at us, and said, "You didn't hold the hand, did you?"

"No," said we; "but we would like to know how you did that." He responded, "I tried to gather a body from the elements; but conditions were not favorable: I could only gather a hand and arm." Now, when this phenomenon is explained, we can explain Jesus' producing hands and feet that could be seen and felt.

We must record one more sentence from Luke concerning Jesus: "And he led them out as far as to Bethany; and he lifted up his hands, and blessed them. And it came to pass, while he blessed them, he was parted from them, and carried up into heaven." — Luke xxiv. 50, 51.

Here Jesus was parted from the disciples in a way that physical bodies are not separated from each other. He was born of the Spirit. John says, "Then the same day, at evening, being the first day of the week, when the doors were shut where the disciples were assembled for fear of the Jews, came Jesus, and stood in the midst, and saith unto them, Peace be unto you; and when he had so said, he showed unto them his hands and his side. Then were the disciples glad, when they saw the Lord" (John xx. 19, 20). Again: "And after eight days, again his disciples were within, and Thomas with them: then came Jesus, the doors being shut, and stood in the midst, and said, Peace be unto you."—Verse 26.

Here the doors were shut against the Jews, fastened to keep them out; but Jesus appeared in the midst of a room fastened to keep intruders out. How does he get there? It is all told in one sentence, He was born of the Spirit; like the wind he could go and come unperceived by mortal vision.

With one more appearance of the man of Nazareth, we will take our leave of this department of this subject.

"And, as he journeyed, he came near Damascus; and suddenly there shined round about him a light from heaven. And he fell to the earth, and heard a voice saying unto him, Saul, Saul, why persecutest thou me? And he said, Who art thou, Lord? And the Lord said, I am Jesus, whom thou persecutest: it is hard for thee to kick against the pricks. And he, trembling and astonished, said, Lord, what wilt thou have me to do? And the Lord said unto him, Arise, and go into the city, and it shall be told thee what thou must do. And the men which journeyed with him stood speechless, hearing a voice, but seeing no man. And Saul arose from the earth; and, when his eyes were opened, he saw no man: but they led him by the hand, and brought him into Damascus." — Acts ix. 3–8.

Here was a spirit-light, here were spirit-voices, and Jesus was seen by Paul, but not by those who were witl him. Paul was one of the "chosen witnesses" to whom "he showed himself alive after his passion." This event occurred several years after the assassination of Jesus. Ananias, in referring to these phenomena, says, —

"Brother Saul, the Lord, even Jesus, that appeared unto thee in the way as thou camest, hath sent me, that thou mightest receive thy sight, and be filled with the Holy Ghost." — Acts ix. 17.

The testimony is positive: what more can be required? Jesus was born of the Spirit. After his appearance on so many occasions, under so many circumstances, and presenting again and again such varied and unmistakable evidence of a life after death, who can but agree with Paul when he says, —

"But is now made manifest by the appearance of our Saviour Jesus Christ, who hath abolished death, and hath brought life and immortality to light through the gospel." — 2 Tim. i. 10.

If his numerous appearances have not been enough to demonstrate immortality to those who saw him, they are beyond the reach of evidence.

If the foregoing is true, and its truth can not be questioned by the believer in the Bible, each one at death is born into another world, — born with the education, ability, and experience obtained in this. Who has not thought, as he has grown old, and worn himself out in learning the lessons of life, "If I could only be placed back to the days of my childhood, with the experience I have gained in this world, what a man I would be by the time I arrived at my present age a second time!" Take, for example, such statesmen as Daniel Webster and Henry Clay, men who spent a lifetime in picking up an education: must such enter the spirit-world as ignorant as an infant of days? Alexander Campbell spent a lifetime in gathering pebbles from the ocean of knowledge, until, finally, he gained the best knowledge of the Bible, its history, the country where it originated, the people among whom it originated, and all connected with it, of any person we ever met who viewed it from his standpoint. When he died, did that knowledge die? Did he live more than eighty years to pick up a few of the lessons of life, and then die and forget all? No. He lived long enough to learn well some things pertaining to man, and then was born again, — born into a better, higher life, in a country where he could use the knowledge he pursued so ardently in this world.

Not only is the resurrection a birth, but all are born into the other life with the peculiarities which attached to them in this. Paul teaches, that as there are different kinds of flesh, as there is one glory of the sun, and another of the moon, as star differeth from star in glory, so is the resurrection of the dead. Daniel says, —

"And they that be wise shall shine as the brightness of the firmament; and they that turn many to righteousness, as the stars for ever and ever." — Dan. xii. 3.

In the world beyond, no one shines with a borrowed light. Each one in the hereafter reflects what his life here makes him there. This is exhibited in no one place as prominently as in spirit manifestations. Take, for example, those in the Bible. Elijah the prophet, while on earth, was always cursing; cursed Ahab, cursed Jezebel, cursed over four hundred of his fellow prophets. He was as perfect a misanthrope as ever lived: he lived the life of a hermit, preferring the society of wild beasts and ravens to men and women. By and by he passed to the spirit-world, and it seemed to be his mission to curse after he got there. The written communication which he gave to King Jehoram seemed to be as full of denunciation as any thing he could have written with his own hand or uttered through his own organism while upon earth. When he influenced John the Baptist, he made him manifest all of his idiosyncrasies, even to that of making his home in the wilderness, and denouncing everybody to whom he preached; insomuch that the Bible hardly needs to state that "he shall go out in the spirit and power of Elias."

We have witnessed the same in modern manifestations. Many have made merry because spirits have influenced modern media, and made them beg for tobacco and whisky; but it is a solemn truth, and one against which we should not close our eyes, that those who are slaves to tobacco and whisky here, must, hereafter, be tormented in the flame of that appetite.

O reader! could you realize this as we see it and know it, you would strive ardently to overcome the baser parts of your nature now. Do, we beseech you, think of the question, Must I, when I return from the "land of the so-called dead," to influence media, make them call for tobacco and whisky? Must I have that longing follow me through many years of spirit-life? Must I be set back years and years in the hereafter by ungoverned appetites and passions? Must I enter the other world a slave to sin, and spend years of eternity in fighting that I never resisted in this life?

Angels help you to realize these things, and assert your manhood now, so that, when the time comes for you to be born into the higher life, you may enter mansions prepared by your daily devotion to duty here.

CHAPTER VI.

ARE WE INFIDELS?

Rapid Growth of Spiritualism — The "Mad-Dog" Cry — Charge ignored — Proceeds from Infidel Hearts — Truths and Errors in the Bible — Dialogue; Minister wants a Bible — All believe Parts, and no one believes All, of the Bible — Illustrative Cases — How shall we decide who the Believers are — The true Test — Works — The Commission — End of the World not yet — Jewish and Christian Age — Preaching, Baptism, and Signs go together — Is Christ in the Church — Signs follow; did Jesus tell the Truth — The Day of Pentecost — Holy Ghost, Definition of — Opinion of Opposers — Peter's Explanation — "What shall we do" — This Power for all — Abrahamic Promise — Holy Ghost for all — Gifts not to cease — Churches acknowledge some of the Gifts — Covet the Best Gifts — When will the Gifts cease — Advice of James — Elijah's Prayer and the Rain; two Positions — Mind will control Matter — All Things under Man — A Lightning-Tamer — Philosophy of Rain — Rain on Battle-Fields, &c. — Yankee Climate-Regulators — Sick Lady — A Dialogue — God not changed by Prayer — Effect of Prayer — Sickness the Result of Sin — Prayer and its Equivalent — Philosophy of Disease and Cure — Impressions Mental and Physical — Philosophy of vomiting — Disease created and removed by Impressions on the Mind — Death from Excitement — Whence the Power of Volition — Spirit-Writing — Cause of Paralysis — Positive and Negative Disease — Philosophy of Controling a Patient — Electric Currents pass from the Nerves of one to another — The Spirit-World supplies the Operator — Author's Experience in healing — Cause of Failures — Jesus sometimes failed — His Disciples do — Author has been healed — Blind see, Deaf hear, &c. — Statement of Abraham Clarke — Letter to "The New-York Dispatch" — Peter Manning's Case — Another Dialogue — The Devil did it — Devil not so good, after all — Another Evidence — Jesus' Logic — Was his Mission divine — Coming of Christ — Symbolic Clouds and Horses — Death has lost its Sting — Challenge — World's Convention.

SPIRITUALISM has stood before the world and claimed a hearing at its bar for twenty-one years. It has, in that space of time, succeeded in getting such a hearing as no other religion has ever obtained. We do not mean that no other religion ever gained such a hearing in twenty-one years as Spiritualism; but we do mean, that, though it is only twenty-one years since the attention of the American people has been called to Spiritualism as a religious system, it now has such a hold of the popular heart as has not been obtained by any other religious system. Indeed, it is the spiritual element contained in the churches and other organizations, that has held them together thus far.

A play is not worthy of going before the public, unless Spiritualism forms an important part of its attractions. A novel must embody Spiritualism in some form, or its publishers will never get their pay for printer's ink and paper. A poem is hardly read, unless, in some manner, it gives utterance to the all-absorbing sentiment of Spiritualism.

Spiritualism has not only made a few millions of converts, but it is working its way into the popular heart as none of the *creedal* systems of the day *can*. *Once* the churches said, "Let it alone! it will die of itself, and scarcely a grease-spot of it will remain." But that grease-spot has spread far and wide through the texture of human life. The "let alone doctrine," as it was called, would not work; and so the churches have decided to imitate the example of the Quaker, who, having a spite against a dog, said, "It is wrong for me to *kill* thee, but I will give thee a *bad name*, and let thee go;" and forthwith he cried out, "*Mad dog!*" so effectually, that *others* pursued the animal and dispatched him.

The mad-dog cry now raised after Spiritualism is "Infidelity." It is now conceded on all hands that Spiritualism can not be killed. Like "Banquo's ghost,"

10

it obstinately refuses to "down," even though bid to do so by churches and ministers. There is no alternative left but to fall in with it, or give reasons for rejecting it. As no reasons can be given that will satisfy the reasoner, the only course left for them is to deal in *ad captandum vulgus:* so they have raised the cry of "Infidelity!"

Spiritualists and Spiritualism have pursued "the even tenor of their ways," paying but little attention to the charges brought against it; knowing that they, for the most part, originate in an incapacity to comprehend its sublime truths.

Now we propose, in this chapter, to review the infidelity charge; and may we commence by saying it is a *slanderous libel*, made, often, for no other purpose than to disguise the infidelity of the heart whence it proceeds? It does happen that persons sometimes think they are looking at others, when they are only looking into a mirror, and seeing themselves reflected. That this is the case with those who accuse Spiritualism of being infidelity, we intend now to prove.

In order to follow out this course, we must have a rule by which the matter may be decided. Such a rule we believe we have found. There is not one person in the world who believes *all* that is contained in the Bible. If we were to take a lighted candle, and search through modern Christianity, we should not find one who believes it *all*. The infidel says, "I do not believe the *errors* in the Bible." — "Neither do *I*," says the Christian. Upon that ground, they meet in common. We read, and all Christians and infidels believe *as* we read, "The grass withereth, the flower thereof faileth;" but, when we see it recorded that Ahaziah was two years older than his *father*, the fact is denied by every one as a natural impossibility. Christians and infidels agree, that a man *can not* be older than his father. Therefore, one of the texts all allow to be true, and the other all reject as false.

The above is sufficient to illustrate that no one believes *all* the Bible. Every one believes *some* of it. How, then, shall we tell who the true believers are?

This case can be illustrated by an incident in our own history. Once upon a time, we engaged in conversation with a minister, who took occasion to admire a copy of the Bible then in our hand, when the following dialogue ensued: —

MINISTER. — "That is a very fine Bible you have, — just such as I have always wanted; but I never could get hold of one. How much will you take for it?"

HULL. — "The book is not for sale. I bought it in Canada for my own use, and I do not know that I could get another without going there for it; and that would be hard to do in these war times."

MIN. — "I will pay you twice what your Bible cost you for it: that will pay you for using a poorer one, or waiting until you can get another like this."

H. — "The truth is, I can not spare this book. I have kept it until it is filled with my own magnetism; and it would be too much like parting with a part of myself."

MIN.— "Now, see here. You don't believe the Bible: why can't you let me have this one?"

H. — "Would you take away the last Bible I have, because I do not believe it? Is there any evidence of the truth of the Bible? If so, where should it be found but in the Bible itself? Surely not in Lardner, Horn, Watson, Paley, or McIlvaine. Where are the evidences of geology but in the earth? To what book but to the starry heavens do you go for your evidences of astronomy? Now, reverse the matter: let me be the believer, and you the unbeliever, and I would give you the book, asking no other reward, only that you would investigate its pages, and try to ascertain their truth. But, my brother, it is easy for one party to accuse another of infidelity. Now, I believe part of the Bible, and part of it I do not believe. Part you believe, and part you do not believe. Parts of it I believe, that you do not; parts of it you believe, that I do not; and parts of it we both believe, and parts of it we both reject."

MIN. — "I do not wish to get into a discussion with you, sir: when you reply to a book which you yourself have written on that subject, it will be time for me to debate with you."

H. — "But the book you ask me to answer admits there are errors in the Bible, and that is all I now claim. There is a text in this Bible which says, —

"'For there are three that bear record in heaven, the Father, the Word, and the Holy Ghost; and these three are one' (1 John v. 7). Do you believe that text?"

MIN. — "No: that is an error. Dr. Clark says it is not in the oldest manuscripts. It was perhaps inserted by St. Augustine, merely as a glossary, but was copied by an ignorant transcriber into the text."

H. — "I am not now inquiring how errors got into that book. You acknowledge this text to be an error, and that is all I claim: so your Christianity and my infidelity are exactly alike on that text. There is another text that says Samuel, after he had been dead some months, said to Saul, 'Why hast thou disquieted me to bring me up?' Do you believe Samuel did visit Saul, and use such words?"

MIN. — "No, I — I — I think — well, the Devil personated Samuel. He is a great deceiver; beside, the Bible plainly says, 'The dead know not any thing.' Samuel, being dead, could not have been there."

H. — "Very well. Your *belief* says the text is false: my *unbelief says it is true.*"

MIN. — "I prefer not to talk with you on these subjects. You know that a positive, 'Thus saith the Bible,' on any subject, in the absence of any other testimony, is not enough to convince you of the truth of a position. It would convince me: so that settles the question."

H. — "Perhaps it does. There is a positive declaration in 2 Kings viii. 26, which says, —

"'Two and twenty years old was Ahaziah when he began to reign; and he reigned one year in Jerusalem. And his mother's name was Athaliah, the daughter of Omri, King of Israel.' Do you believe that?"

MIN. — "Let me see that text. Yes: the Bible says so, and I believe it. Do you believe it?"

H. — "I do not know whether I believe it or not."

MIN. — "There, that fixes the whole question. You acknowledge the Bible reads just as you have quoted; but, because you have no corroborative evidence, you do not know as you believe it. I know it is true, because the Bible says so."

H. — "Here is another text I will ask you if you believe. It says, —

"'*Forty* and *two* years old was Ahaziah when he began

to reign, and he reigned one year in Jerusalem. His mother's name also was Athaliah, the daughter of Omri' (2 Chron. xxii. 2). Do you believe that?"

MIN.—"Wha—wha—what does that text say? Let me see it."

H.—"It says he was *forty-two* years old at the time the other text sets him down at *twenty-two*. He could not have been forty-two and twenty-two at the same time; and you have committed yourself *to* the former text: in doing so, you committed yourself *against* the latter; so your amount of fidelity over mine in one instance is made up by your amount of *infidelity* over mine in the other. The statement concerning Jehoram, the father of Ahaziah, is,—

"'Thirty and two years old was he when he began to reign; and he reigned in Jerusalem eight years, and departed without being desired.'—2 Chron. xxi. 20.

"Now, if Jehoram reigned eight years, and was thirty-two at his ascending the throne, he was only *forty* years old at his death; and his youngest son, Ahaziah, was forty-two: that makes the youngest son only two years older than his father. There are a great many sons in 'Young America' more than that much older than their parents."

This minister was "one of a thousand." It will always be found that the man who believes so much of the Bible, and finds nothing but infidelity in the opinions of others, is one who either has no comprehension of the opinions of others, or knows but little of what the Bible contains. Now, since no one believes *all* of the Bible, and every one believes *some* of it, how will it be settled as to who the believers are? Shall we tell them by the length of their prayers, or by the length of their faces? Will their having attached their name to a religious creed be sufficient to prove them believers, or must we decide by the sacredness they attach to certain days of the week, or the rigor with which they enforce certain religious ceremonies? None of these rules will do. There are thousands of baptized infidels to-day.

Jesus has laid down a rule by which to test this matter. He says, —

"Verily, verily, I say unto you, He that believeth on me, the works that I do shall he do also; and greater works than these shall he do, because I go unto my Father."— John xiv. 12.

This language can not easily be misinterpreted. Jesus set out to tell us who believers are. He does not test them by their *professions*, by *forms* or *ceremonies*, but by their *works*. Christians, are you willing to be tested thus? "*He that believeth shall do the works that I do;*" yea, even *greater works*. Did Jesus, or did he not, tell the truth? Do you, or do you not, believe? Will you do yourselves the favor to heed Paul's admonition? —

"Examine yourselves, whether ye be in the faith; prove your own selves." — 2 Cor. xiii. 5.

James says, —

"Yea, a man may say, Thou hast faith, and I have works; show me thy faith without thy works, and I will show thee my faith by my works." — James ii. 18.

These Scriptures can not be misunderstood. You are not only admonished to "prove yourselves," but told how, — show your faith by your works. What works? "The works that I do, and even greater, shall he do."

We ask again, Do you believe? Oh, would that we had the power to ring the question in every ear!

After Jesus' *anastasis*, he said to his disciples, —

"Go ye therefore, and teach all nations, baptizing them in the name of the Father, and of the Son, and of the Holy Ghost, teaching them to observe all things whatsoever I have commanded you; and lo, I am with you alway, even unto the end of the world." — Matt. xxviii. 19, 20.

Here Christ promised to be with his disciples. This means something. He is not going to be with them and not make himself manifest. The only way the Church can know that Christ is with them is by certain manifestations. Mark records the fulfillment of this promise in his day as follows: —

"And they went forth, and preached everywhere, the Lord working with them, and confirming the word with signs following." — Mark xvi. 20.

When Paul and Barnabas preached at Iconium, Luke says, —

"Long time, therefore, abode they, speaking boldly in the Lord, which gave testimony unto the word of his grace, and granted signs and wonders to be done by their hands." — Acts xiv. 3.

The text does not promise to be with the disciples merely to the end of their generation, but "*always, even to the end of the world.*" Though many are looking for the end of the world very soon, and almost innumerable times have been set for old Father Time to cease his rounds, he, not daunted in the least by the notices that he will cease to bring the seasons around, trudges along as usual. Then Christ is to work with his disciples yet, or the text is not true. Does he do it? Is there a church to-day that has the signs by which to prove that Christ is with it? Said a minister to us, "If the word 'world' signified all time, as you seem to think, your remarks would be just; but the Greek word *aion*, rendered 'world' in this instance, only signifies age or dispensation. This language was used in the Jewish, and not in the Christian age: therefore it only means that Christ will be with his disciples to the end of the Jewish dispensation." "When did the Jewish age end, and the Christion age commence?" we asked. "On the day of Pentecost," was his reply. Very well, the preaching did not commence until the day of Pentecost. They were not to set out immediately on their mission. Luke says, that Jesus, after giving their commission to preach, said, —

"And, behold, I send the promise of my Father upon you; but tarry ye in the city of Jerusalem until ye be endued with power from on high." — Luke xxiv. 49.

This enduement came on the day of Pentecost, the very time where the beginning of the Christian dispensation is located. Jesus is to work with his disciples to the end of the dispensation where the preaching is to be done. Is the command to preach binding yet? and are persons now baptized in obedience to this text? Then, if Jesus is not with the Church to-day, it is either because he did not tell the truth, or its members are infidels.

A representative of modern infidelity, falsely called theology, informed us that Christ was with the Church until it was established: from that time forward, he had not been with it. This was admitting the whole ground: their Church was composed of Christless infidels!

Mark represents Jesus as saying, —

"And these signs shall follow them that believe: in my name shall they cast out devils; they shall speak with new tongues; they shall take up serpents, and, if they drink any deadly thing, it shall not hurt them; they shall lay hands on the sick, and they shall recover." — Mark xvi. 17, 18.

Here again the language is positive and emphatic. "These signs *shall* follow them that believe." There is no proviso in the case. Do the signs follow those who accuse Spiritualists of infidelity? If not, are they not, when they make such charges, speaking of the abundance of their own infidel hearts?

The disciples were requested to tarry at Jerusalem until they were endued with power from on high. They did so. On the fortieth day after they first saw Jesus after his martyrdom, they saw him for the last time. They then formed what Spiritualists call a *circle* in an upper room in the city; and there they sat for ten days, waiting for this power. At the end of that time, they began to have manifestations, such as are of common occurrence among modern Spiritualists. The writer of the Book of Acts describes it thus: —

"And, when the day of Pentecost was fully come, they were all with one accord in one place. And suddenly there came a sound from heaven as of a rushing mighty wind, and it filled all the house where they were sitting. And there appeared unto them cloven tongues like as of fire, and it sat upon each of them. And they were all filled with the Holy Ghost, and began to speak with other tongues, as the Spirit gave them utterance. And there were dwelling at Jerusalem Jews, devout men, out of every nation under heaven. Now when this was noised abroad, the multitude came together, and were confounded, because that every man heard them speak in his own language. And they were all amazed, and marveled, saying one to another, Behold, are not all these which speak Galileans? And how hear we every man in our own tongue, wherein we were born?" — Acts ii. 1–8.

Here is a foreign power lighting upon the disciples in cloven, or a diversity of tongues, literally *split* tongues; that is, tongues that speak a number of languages. These illiterate Galilean fishermen fluently speak seventeen different languages, not one of which they understand. The power thus using these mediums is called "the Holy Ghost;" that is, *pneumatos hagion*. One of the definitions which Greenfield gives the word *pneumatos* is "human souls;" and we know of no better definition of the word *hagion* than "good." A "spirit power lights upon them, that the Bible designates as the good spirit." Whose spirit it was we do not know. Of two things we are sure: first, it fulfills the Christ prediction, "I am with you;" second, it was just such a power as works on modern media.

These manifestations of course astonish the people, who were worshiping dead forms and ceremonies, instead of having any living evidence of their religion.

"And they were all amazed, and were in doubt, saying one to another, What meaneth this? Others, mocking, said, These men are full of new wine." — Acts ii. 12, 13.

This last charge brings Peter to his feet. Here the gospel commences: —

"Ye men of Judæa, and all ye that dwell at Jerusalem, be this known unto you, and hearken to my words; for these are not drunken, as ye suppose, seeing it is but the third hour of the day. But this is that which was spoken by the prophet Joel: And it shall come to pass in the last days, saith God, I will pour out of my Spirit upon all flesh; and your sons and your daughters shall prophesy, and your young men shall see visions, and your old men shall dream dreams: and on my servants and on my handmaidens I will pour out in those days of my Spirit; and they shall prophesy." — Acts ii. 14–18.

This is a complete refutation of those Jewish rabbis. Peter thoroughly exposes their theory of the men being under the influence of wine. It was too early an hour. The wine they drank then was not such drink as men indulge in now-a-days. Men could drink all day, and by nightfall they would begin to be intoxicated: hence the proverb, "They that are drunken, are drunken in the night." Beside, wine does not teach men seventeen different languages they never heard. After refuting the position of these exposers of ancient spirit-manifestations, Peter proceeds to state his own, which is, that this is a fulfillment of a certain prediction. His reasonings so perfectly commend themselves to the people, that they are convinced, and at once cry out, "What shall we do?" Do for what? we ask. "To be saved," nearly the whole world responds. Not a bit of it. They, in this question, had no more idea of salvation than they had of going into Noah's ark. No: they had witnessed certain *phenomena;* and they were interested in knowing how they could be produced. Now the question is, What shall we do to have the power manifest here? Peter's answer is pertinent: —

"Then Peter said unto them, Repent, and be baptized, every one of you, in the name of Jesus Christ for the remission of sins, *and ye shall receive the gift of the Holy Ghost. For the promise is unto you, and to your children, and to all that are afar off, even as many as the Lord our God shall call.*" — Acts ii. 38, 39.

It was the gift of the Holy Ghost that enabled the disciples to work the wonders which were exciting the people. Now, Peter tells them they can have the same power on certain conditions: "for the promise is to them; not to them only, but to their children; and not them alone, but all that are afar off, even as many as the Lord our God shall call."

A kind friend once volunteered to enlighten us upon this subject. "This promise made to them and their children *et al.*," said he, "was the Abrahamic promise." The promise made to Abraham was in the following words: —

"And the Lord said unto Abram, after that Lot was separated from him, Lift up now thine eyes, and look from the place where thou art, northward and southward, and eastward and westward; for all the land which thou seest, to thee will I give it, and to thy seed for ever. And I will make thy seed as the dust of the earth, so that, if a man can number the dust of the earth, then shall thy seed also be numbered." — Gen. xiii. 14–16.

What reference this text could have to this promise it would take at least a divine to imagine. No: here is the promise: —

"Therefore being by the right hand of God exalted, and having received of the Father the promise of the Holy Ghost, he hath shed forth this, which ye now see and hear." — Acts ii. 33.

Now, this promise of the Holy Ghost *is to all who are called;* but the Holy Ghost enables those under its power to do what was done on the day of Pentecost.

"But," says the objector, "these signs were to cease." Then all the Scriptures quoted in this chapter thus far are false. Here we venture the assertion, that not an argument, except the fact that the churches do not enjoy the gifts, can be brought to prove that they should have ceased: that, instead of proving the gifts should cease, proves the relapse of the Church into infidelity. Churches themselves do not believe in the cessation of all the gifts. In Rom. xii. 6–8, Paul says, —

"Having, then, gifts differing according to the grace that is given us, whether prophecy, let us prophesy according to the proportion of faith; or ministry, let us wait on our ministering; or he that teacheth, on teaching, or he that exhorteth, on exhortation: he that giveth, let him do it with simplicity; he that ruleth, with diligence; he that showeth mercy, with cheerfulness."

The gifts all go together; yet the Church denies the gift of prophecy, and acknowledges that of the ministry, teaching, and exhortation.

In 1 Cor. xii. 7–11, Paul says, "But the manifestation of the Spirit is given to every man to profit withal. For to one is given by the Spirit the word of wisdom; to another, the word of knowledge by the same Spirit; to another, faith by the same Spirit; to another, the gifts of healing by the same Spirit; to another, the working of miracles; to another, prophecy; to another, discerning of spirits; to another, divers kinds of tongues; to another, the interpretation of tongues: but all these worketh that one and the selfsame Spirit, dividing to every man severally as he will."

Does Paul tell the truth? If so, every man is entitled to some form of the manifestation of the Spirit. One would think, by the way opposition to spirit-manifestations rages in the Church, that that, too, was a gift of the Spirit. Here, this Spirit that gives the power to teach and preach the word to one gives to another the power to heal the sick; to another, the power to prophesy; another, the power to work miracles (marvels); another, the discerning (seeing and describing) of spirits; and to another, the power to speak in foreign languages.

But Paul continues: "And God hath set some in the church; first apostles, secondarily prophets, thirdly teachers; after that miracles; then gifts of healings, helps, governments, diversities of tongues. Are all apostles? are all prophets? are all teachers? are all workers of miracles? have all the gifts of healing? do all speak with tongues? do all interpret? But covet earnestly the best gifts; and yet show I unto you a more excellent way."—1 Cor. xii. 28–31.

The Church now has its teachers, helps, and governments; then why deny it the other gifts mentioned in this chapter, which it has an equal right to claim? Nay, why charge infidelity upon the only people in the world who, by the exercise of spiritual powers, prove themselves legitimate Christians?

In chap. xiv. 1, Paul admonishes his brethren to "follow after charity, and *desire spiritual gifts*."

But the Church, having lost both charity and gifts, spends its time in ardently wishing others were in equally as doleful a situation. Truly, the words of the Judæan reformer, "The kingdom shall be taken from you, and given to a nation bringing forth the fruits thereof," are more literally fulfilled than many imagine. Verse twelve of this same chapter, instead of teaching that the gifts shall cease, admonishes Christians to "be zealous of spiritual gifts, and seek to excel."

"But there is a text somewhere," said an objector, "that teaches that the gifts shall cease." Yes: there is just one. Here it is: —

"Charity never faileth; but, whether there be prophecies, they shall fail; whether there be tongues, they shall cease; whether there be knowledge, it shall vanish away. For we know in part, and we prophesy in part. But, when that which is perfect is come, then that which is in part shall be done away." — 1 Cor. xiii. 7–10.

Here the matter is stated clearly. "When that which is perfect is come, then that which is in part shall be done away." When

> "Hope shall change to glad fruition,
> Faith to sight, and prayer to praise,"

then, and not till then, will the gifts cease. While there are sick, the gift of healing will remain; while persons do not all understand one language, the power to speak in others will remain. Until then, if the gifts cease, it is because of infidelity.

We will now turn our attention to one particular department of this subject. We will select that of healing. James says, —

"Is any sick among you? let him call for the elders of the church; and let them pray over him, anointing him with oil in the name of the Lord. And the prayer of faith shall save the sick, and the Lord shall raise him up; and, if he have committed sins, they shall be forgiven him." — James v. 14, 15.

Christians, you who take the Bible for the rule of your faith and practice, do you follow James's injunction? Will you? Dare you undertake to show your faith by your works? James did not counsel to send for a doctor: an ancient Christian would as soon think of sending for a lawyer as a doctor. "Send for the elders," is the injunction; let them pray for him: the prayer of faith shall save the sick. Is there faith enough in all professed Christendom to save one patient?

But James continues to argue the case: —

"Elias was a man subject to like passions as we are, and he prayed earnestly that it might not rain; and it rained not on the earth by the space of three years and six months. And he prayed again, and the heaven gave rain, and the earth brought forth her fruit." — James v. 17, 18.

James's argument in reference to the sick is based on the fact that Elijah controlled the elements. This he did, or the statement made here, and in 1 Kings xvii. 1, is not true. There is only one of two ways in which this could have been done: first, by interceding with an especial power which controls the elements; or, second, working in harmony with some law which produced such an effect. In either case, the power that can control the elements so as to regulate the falling of rain can certainly control enough to drive disease from the human system. If James argues that it was done as an especial favor in answer to prayer, then his position is, God will hear prayer as in the case of Elias; otherwise, his position is, man can control the elements as in the case of Elijah.

The world is now beginning to understand that mind must control matter. Man will yet control all the elements. This idea is found in more than one place in the Bible. David says of man, —

"Thou madest him to have dominion over the works of thy hands; thou hast put all things under his feet." — Ps. viii. 6.

Paul quotes and comments on this text as follows: —

"But one in a certain place testified, saying, What is man, that thou art mindful of him? or the son of man, that thou visitest him? Thou madest him a little lower than the angels; thou crownedst him with glory and honor, and didst set him over the works of thy hands. Thou hast put all things in subjection under his feet. For, in that he put all in subjection under him, he left nothing that is not put under him. But now we see not yet all things put under him." — Heb. ii. 6–8.

So it is. All things — yea, all the elements — are, *prospectively*, under man; but all things are not yet, *in fact*, under his control. As man obtains a knowledge of science, the elements, one after another, become subject to him. We do believe, with James, David, and Paul, that man will yet control them all.

"My friend," said a good mother in Israel to us, "that is blasphemy. You talk of making it rain: that is taking God's business out of his hands. You must not assume to be God." "Yes," said we: "there are a great many blasphemers in the world. In the last century, there was one, Benjamin Franklin by name, who undertook to take the lightning out of the hands of the Almighty, and succeeded; corked it up in a bottle, carried it in his pocket, and exhibited it as a trophy of the triumph of science. The world which scoffed and laughed at the 'insane blasphemer,' at once began to worship him as a semi-god. If the lightning, the most subtile of all the elements, can be even partially controlled by man, certainly the grosser elements can be made to yield to his power."

There are laws regulating the falling of rain; and man needs but to understand and apply them to produce a shower. Every one knows, that, if a lump of ice be put into a pitcher of water on a very hot day, the result will be, that water will soon cover the whole outside of the pitcher. The philosophy of the phenomenon is simply this: the atmosphere outside of the pitcher is warm; the cold water and ice inside the pitcher change the temperature; the vessel, being a conductor, conveys the cold temperature to its surface; there it meets the heated atmosphere; and the result is a condensation; the hydrogen of the atmosphere in immediate connection with the vessel settles upon it. Thus a small shower has been produced. Apply this law on a larger scale, and a heavier rain-storm is the result. Rains have almost always followed as a result of hard battles, where there was a great deal of heavy cannonading. It has been remarked in this country that a shower is more apt to come up on the afternoon of the fourth day of July than any other day of that month. The celebration on that day of our nation's birth, which is done by burning powder and jarring up the elements, is undoubtedly the cause. Atmosphere, as it is heated and disturbed, expands, and, of course, in proportion to its bulk, becomes lighter; the result is, it rises, and the colder, heavier atmosphere sinks; as the heated air rises through the cold, the condensation occurs; and, as a result, we have a shower of rain.

Now, we venture to say, give a Yankee a furnace of sufficient magnitude to heat a sufficient portion of air, and an engine of sufficient power to send the heated atmosphere through the colder stratum, and he will produce a shower any time on twenty-four hours' notice.

If it were possible to bore down five miles into the earth, we would find a heat sufficient to melt the hardest substance known. May not the time come when man will be able to dive down into the bowels of the earth, and from its eternal fire regulate our climate, both as to temperature and moisture? But if the elements can be controlled, as James insinuates, why may not the other portion of the text be true, and disease pass under the control of man?

Permit us now to examine this from a scientific standpoint. And, first, we must inquire after the philosophy of disease and cure. To illustrate: suppose a lady, the mother of four children, to be taken ill. She decides to send for the elder, as per direction, and have him pray for her. A philosopher chances to meet the elder at the lady's house, and the following dialogue ensues: —

PHILOSOPHER. — "What is the cause of the lady's sickness?"

ELDER. — "Ah! 'the Lord hath greatly afflicted her.' You know that

'God moves in a mysterious way
His wonders to perform:
He plants his footsteps in the sea,
And rides upon the storm!'"

PHIL. — "Why has God afflicted her?"

ELD. — "Because, in his wisdom, he sees it to be the best."

PHIL. — "Then why pray for it to be removed? If it is best for her to be afflicted, do not ask God to remove that which she needs. The superior wisdom of the Almighty knows that she needs affliction: hence he has sent it upon her. Now, will you ask Infinite Wisdom to give place to your folly, and heal her, when he knows that it is not for the best? and will he obey you? That makes God a time-serving demagogue, whiffling about to suit the thousand and one notions of his creatures. When you prove that position, I will cease to believe the world is governed by Infinite Wisdom, but by the caprices of his people: so, if God has afflicted the lady, my advice to you is to let him manage the matter. What did God make her sick for?"

ELD. — "Oh! he intends to take her to himself."

PHIL. — "He does? Well, he is abundantly able to carry out his determinations. He undoubtedly thinks it is best that she should die, or he would not kill her; and if God, who, you will admit, ought to know, thinks it best that she should die, I will not ask him to revoke his decision to take her life: for, the moment he yields to my judgment, he is *un-God*-ed."

Eld. — " She has four children, who will be left without a mother. It is a pity that she should die: I will tell God all, and ask him to restore her."

Phil. — ' Then you think, when you lay all the facts before the Author of the universe, that he may *reconsider* the case. Perhaps he has not thought that these children will be left in so destitute a condition."

Eld. — " Well, the fact is, I do not think we can change the mind of the omnipotent God; but I will ask him, if it is in harmony with his will, to raise her up. I think he intends to restore her to health."

Phil. — " Very well: if he intends to restore her, he will accomplish it. Why do you interfere? If the lady is restored to health, it is in accordance with the predetermination of God, and not in answer to your prayers."

Eld. — " You must be an infidel: don't you believe in praying for the sick?"

Phil. — " I most certainly believe in praying for the afflicted; but convince me that God has any thing to do with the matter, one way or another, and I will never pray. God is abundantly able to attend to his own business."

Eld. — " What do you mean? Has God nothing to do with the case?"

Phil. — " Nothing at all. The lady has violated the laws of health, and is now paying the penalty. Jesus, if he were to administer to her needs, would say, ' Daughter, thy sins are forgiven thee.' Sin, a violation of the law, and nothing else, has made her sick. ' God, in his providence,' does not send dyspepsia to one who has not been intemperate either in the quantity or quality of food and drink taken into the stomach. I have known many dyspeptics to charge to God what they owed to greed. Rheumatism and all the ailments of mankind come as the result of sin against the laws of health; and all that is wanted to remove disease is to restore the broken laws."

ELD. — "But will prayer do it?"

PHIL. — "In many instances, it will. It would do it in almost every case in the days of James; and now, in cases where prayer will not remove disease, there is an equivalent in something else."

ELD. — "What is it? I do not understand you."

PHIL. — "I will explain. Disease is under the control of mind, — partially the mind of the operator, and partially, it may be, the mind of the patient. In order to effectually remove disease, the patient must be not only negative to the operator, but in magnetic *rapport* with him: so, if the one to be healed is a great believer in prayer, her confidence is inspired, and she passes into more perfect communion with the operator by that than by any other means. If, on the other hand, the patient is a philosopher, largely developed in the region of causality and comparison, he will be disgusted with the insane verbiage generally handed out as prayer; and his disgust, if nothing else, will cause him to repel all the health-giving power, which, otherwise, might have been imparted. In such a case, three minutes of philosophy would be worth more than three months of prayer; for, be it understood, the power must pass from the operator to the patient."

ELD. — "This may be infidelity, but it is strangely interesting: please proceed."

Phil. — " Disease and cure are always the result of impression, — sometimes mental and sometimes physical. There are cases where it is necessary to produce a physical impression in order to operate on the mental faculties. It is well known that lobelia will produce vomiting. The philosophy is this: lobelia is a foreign substance, does not belong to the stomach. As soon as it is thrown into it, the whole system learns there is an unlawful tenant there, and sends its fluids to neutralize it: the stomach cramps, has spasms, and, as a result, disgorges its contents. In this case, vomiting was produced as a result of a physical impression. Now, this effect could be produced by producing a *mental* impression. Make the patient *know*, *beyond a doubt*, that he has taken any kind of medicine, and the same result as though he had taken the medicine will follow. Speak to a very sensitive lady in a positive manner, so as to make her believe, beyond a doubt, that she has swallowed a fly, and vomiting will be the result. The stomach will not retain a fly; and the effect of making a person believe that a fly is in the stomach is the same as though it was there. Criminals condemned to death have been put on clean, nice beds, and been made to believe that persons had recently died with small-pox on the beds on which they were to sleep: the result was, they took the contagion, and died. In hundreds of instances, mental impressions have created disease by which patients have lost their lives. A man was once lying on his back, unable to move, from inflammatory rheumatism, when he saw his father fall from the top of a cherry-tree in the yard, and, he supposed, kill himself. The invalid jumped from his helpless position, and picked up his father, and carried him into the house, and was perfectly surprised to find himself restored to health."

ELD. — "What removed his disease?"

PHIL. — "The excitement of the occasion. Now, man should look from such phenomena to the law which produces them, and he might apply it with beneficial results."

Our philosopher is correct. The excitement started the electric fluid, and that started all the fluids of the system into action: the result was a complete change for the better. We personally knew of an individual, who held a county office by the suffrage of the people, who went to a political meeting of the party whose sentiments he did not indorse; and upon being called a liar, knave, and villain, and accused of stealing, and several other such crimes as politicians usually accuse the party in power of committing, the individual became so excited, that he took an apoplectic fit, and died. Whatever doctors and coroner's juries may have decided, this man was killed by the abuse heaped on him by the speaker. Now, the law by which this man was killed might be used in many cases (perhaps not to so great an extent as was here used) with beneficial results. There are thousands of hypochondriacs to-day who need nothing more than to have their anger thoroughly aroused to effect a cure. The system can not remain diseased where the electric fluid flows properly; and, where it does not, disease must be the result.

Will some philosopher tell the power by which our pen now moves in obedience to our will? All acknowledge that *somehow* mind is the propelling power. All volition inheres in mind or spirit. The mind wills the pen to move; but the mind can not operate upon the pen without a medium: it uses the hand as the medium by which to move the pen. But the mind can not touch the hand: it must operate on something it can touch. The muscle can operate on the bones of the hand, and all other bones; but the mind can not operate on the muscle: the blood, however, can. Now, all would be right if the mind could operate on the blood; but that it can not do. The nerves, or rather the electric currents flowing through the nerves, can operate on the blood; and the mind operates directly on these currents. Hence we have it as follows: the mind, or spirit, which has its throne in the brain, which is but the termination of all the nerves of the system, operates on electricity, uses it as its agent; the electricity operates on the nerves, the nerves on the blood, the blood on the muscle, the muscle on the bone, the bone on the pen, and thus the spirit writes. If other spirits could become positive to the spirit controlling this organism, they could control this spirit, and through it the entire organism.

Now suppose, while writing, our pen suddenly drops from our hand, and the hand to our side, totally paralyzed: where is the disease? No scalpel can find it. Cut the body into inch pieces, and the right side, though utterly unable to move, would, to all appearances, be found as healthy as the other. Then why does not the right hand move as well as the left? We answer, When the mind wishes the hand to move, it *telegraphs* from its office in the brain along these nerves to the hand to move; and the hand always does its bidding. But when there is an obstruction in the nerves, so the electricity can not flow, the hand can not receive the dispatch, and hence can not know that it has been requested to move. Remove the obstruction from the nerves, so that the electricity can flow properly, and all is well.

All disease is either positive or negative, and always lights on the weakest part of the patient. Load a wagon too heavily, and the weakest part will break: so, if a person is weaker in the knees than the lungs, his disease may be inflammatory rheumatism; if weakest in the lungs, it may be lung fever; if, perchance, the kidneys are the weakest, all other portions of the organism might escape, and the patient be afflicted with inflammation in those organs. If the currents flow too rapidly, the disease is positive; and the result is fever, acute pain, and sometimes insanity. If, on the other hand, the currents do not flow rapidly enough, the result will be cold extremities, dull, stupid feelings, partial or total paralysis, &c. In either instance, all that is needed is to set the currents of electricity into proper action. How can this be done? As our philosopher intimated, sometimes by prayer, sometimes by anger, and sometimes by excitement.

In order to remove or control the disease of a patient, the operator must at least have a partial control of the electric currents of the system: those he can control by controlling the mind of the patient; and that must be done by the electric currents of his own system. These currents, especially so far as the voluntary organs are concerned, must be under the control of his will-power: he must by will-power overcome the will of the patient; to do this, the patient must be kept in a receptive or negative condition. This is easily done by gaining and retaining the confidence of the patient; so, if the patient is a great believer in prayer, the surest method will be to pray. If not, some other means must be devised.

The electric currents flowing through the nerves can be made to pass through the nerves of any number of persons by their joining hands. Witness where a dozen or more form a circle, and those at the ends hold on to a battery, all in the circle will receive the same shock at the same time. The nerves of those having hold of the latter are filled with electricity; and electric currents, like all things else, seek their equilibrium, and hence infill the nerves of all who are in contact with those in connection with the battery. Now, let patient and operator come in contact, either mental or physical, and the electric currents at once seek an equilibrium: when that has been obtained, the cause of disease has been removed. Now, in proportion to the operator's mediumship, he is interwoven with a circle of spirits, who can impart to him the needed life and health giving influences; and in proportion as he passes into magnetic *rapport* with his patients, will they be brought into connection with a health-imparting influence from the beyond. This we know, both as a matter of science and history. Having spent near six years in the study and practice of this mediumship, our faith takes hold of the wonderful cures wrought by prophets, Jesus, and his comrades of olden time. We know there is a law by which such things are being done now: that law, being as old as heaven, reaches back over the first case of healing, and is more eternal than the "everlasting hills."

We frankly confess, that, in our healing efforts, we

have failed to perform a perfect cure in three cases out of five; but does that prove there is nothing in this mediumship, or that it has not been vouchsafed to us? No: it only proves that in cases of failure we did not get *en rapport*, either with the *fountains* whence we drew our supply, or with the patient to whom we humbly sought to impart the needed blessing. The best healers in the world fail sometimes. It was so anciently; and it is so to-day. Jesus often failed. In his own country, his brethren became offended with him: the result was such an antagonism that he could not do any thing. The Evangelist says, —

"And they were offended with him. But Jesus said unto them, A prophet is not without honor, save in his own country and in his own house. And he did not many mighty works there, because of their unbelief." — Matt. xiii. 57, 58.

In Mark vi. 4–6, we read, —

"But Jesus said unto them, A prophet is not without honor, but in his own country, and among his own kin, and in his own house. And he could there do no mighty work, save that he laid his hands upon a few sick folk, and healed them. And he marveled because of their unbelief. And he went round about the villages teaching."

In Mark ix. 17–29, we have a full history of the failure of Jesus' disciples in one case, and of his statement as to the cause. Even after the young man was healed, the friends pronounced him dead. In this case, Jesus would not operate until he saw that the father, who was *en rapport* with the patient, with tears in his eyes avowed his entire confidence in the healing power of the Nazarene. The case is so interesting, we give it entire: —

"And one of the multitude answered and said, Master, I have brought unto thee my son, which hath a dumb spirit: and wheresoever he taketh him he teareth him; and he foameth, and gnasheth with his teeth, and pineth away; and I spake to thy disciples, that they should cast him out; and they could not. He answereth him, and saith, O faithless generation! how long shall I be with you? how long shall I suffer you? bring him unto me. And they brought him unto him: and when he saw him, straightway the spirit tare him; and he fell on the ground and wallowed foaming. And he asked his father, How long is it ago since this came unto him? And he said, Of a child. And oft-times it hath cast him into the fire, and into the waters, to destroy him; but, if thou canst do any thing, have compassion on us, and help us. Jesus said unto him, If thou canst believe, all things are possible to him that believeth. And straightway the father of the child cried out, and said with tears, Lord, I believe: help thou mine unbelief. When Jesus saw that the people came running together, he rebuked the foul spirit, saying unto him, Thou dumb and deaf spirit, I charge thee, come out of him, and enter no more into him. And the spirit cried, and rent him sore, and came out of him; and he was as one dead, insomuch that many said, He is dead. But Jesus took him by the hand, and lifted him up; and he arose. And when he was come into the house, his disciples asked him privately, Why could not we cast him out? And he said unto them, This kind can come forth by nothing but by prayer and fasting."

This case is sufficient to show that in ancient times, where one medium failed to remove disease, another could sometimes afford the needed relief.

In this chapter we have briefly gone through the New Testament, and shown that believers should exercise the same power Jesus used. We have also shown, from science, the probabilities that such things should occur. It remains, that we present a few historical facts, showing that the Christ-power is yet on the earth. We have so often been relieved of distress in our own person, and have on so many occasions witnessed it in others, that it would take a larger volume than the one we are writing to hold every narrative we could bring. From the hands of Dr. J. R. Newton of Boston, Dr. J. P. Bryant of New York, Drs. Freeman and Wilbur of Milwaukee, we have experienced such sudden and perfect relief, that we could not question the power. We have seen persons, within five minutes of the time they have hobbled into the presence of Dr. Newton or Bryant, on crutches, leave their crutches, and go away perfectly well, in many instances "leaping, and praising God." We have witnessed the opening of blind eyes, and have heard tongues long silent lisp the praise of the power by which they were loosed. We, ourself, have, by the word or touch, cured nearly every ailment that overtakes the flesh.

A few statements from those who have been healed may not come amiss here. We have seen an autograph letter, of which the following is a true copy: —

INDIANAPOLIS, IND., NOV. 30, 1868.

DR. J. R. NEWTON. *Dear Sir,* — Duty impels me to give you a plain statement of my life's sufferings, and cure by you; which you may publish.

I, Abraham Clarke, of Indianapolis, Ind., twenty-one years old the 25th inst., having been a paralytic cripple ever since I was three months old, unable even to lift my hands up to my head, or walk without great difficulty, and so nervous I could hardly stand or sit still, and at times suffering so great pain that my wailings were intolerable to those around me, on Saturday last, Nov. 28, went with my mother to see if you could cure me; for I had heard so much of your wonderful power of curing all kinds of diseases, without medicine, which all other doctors said were incurable, that I had faith you could.

To make a short story, I say, *you cured me perfectly*, with one treatment. I arose upon my feet, walked without limping, with a firm, easy step, raised my hands above my head; then I took a large, heavy chair in either hand by the leg of each, holding and balancing them above my head as few well men can do. And, to sum it all up, I say that I am made whole and sound as any other living man, as far as I know or others discern, and for the first time in my life am in the full enjoyment of health. And I thank my heavenly Father that I am a well man. My former life and suffering seem like a dream.

In gratitude, I am your friend,

ABRAHAM CLARKE.

INDIANAPOLIS, Nov. 30, 1868.

Personally appeared before me Abraham Clarke, who deposes under oath that the foregoing statement is every word true.

Subscribed and sworn before me, J. P. Pinkerton, a Notary Public, in and for the County of Marion, State of Indiana.

J. P. PINKERTON, *Notary Public.*

The foregoing statement of my son, Abraham Clarke, is all true. ISABELLA CLARKE.

Dr. Newton is now operating at No. 23 Harrison Avenue, Boston, where there are on exhibition faithful photographic likenesses of this young man, taken immediately before and after his treatment: the difference in his looks could not be imagined by one who had not seen them.

The following we copy from "The New-York Dispatch:" —

A JUST TRIBUTE TO DR. J. R. NEWTON.

NEW YORK, Oct. 2

DEAR SIR, — Having seen in "The Tribune" of Sept. 10 an account of "Healing by Magnetism," I can not, in justice to Dr. Newton or to my own feelings, refrain from giving a true statement of the most wonderful and impressive scene that I have ever witnessed in my life of nearly fifty years. The daughter of my brother, a farmer residing in New Boston, N.H., has, for the past three years, been one of the greatest sufferers, and for six years an invalid, suffering from spinal disease and other ailments. Her father has labored by day and night to secure for her the services of eleven of the best physicians in the neighborhood of his home: but her disease has defied their utmost efforts and skill: and they had left her to linger and die, declaring they could do no more for her.

The father, in agony of heart, wrote me that he knew not what to do. Deeply sympathizing with him, and being about to visit some friends in Vermont, I wrote to inform him that I had heard of one Dr. J. R. Newton (but I had never seen him), who was reported to have performed some wonderful cures; and if his daughter wished to come, and could bear the journey of two hundred and fifty miles, and would write me while in Vermont, I would go to his house, and bring her home with me to see Dr. Newton. The answer was in the affirmative, and I went to see my niece; but when I entered the chamber of the sick girl, and looked upon her wan and emaciated body, that had wasted, since I last saw her, from one hundred and twenty-five pounds to less than seventy; when I recollected that she had lain in that situation for two long years, depending for every motion upon kind and gentle hands, my faith left me: I did not believe she could be moved, much less cured.

She was, however, willing and anxious to make the attempt; and when we laid her carefully upon a narrow bed, and carried her down stairs, and placed her in a carriage to ride eighteen miles to the cars, it seemed the height of folly to start on such an undertaking with such a charge, with such a faint hold on human life. When she reached the cars, she said it seemed as though all her strength was gone, and that she could not live much longer. She was, however, restored by the use of stimulants; and we went on. She was taken one hundred and seventeen miles by railroad, and one hundred and fifteen by steamboat, and arrived in New York on the morning of Aug. 30. The patient had suffered intensely through the whole of the journey. It was with great difficulty that she was carried on a stretcher to the house of her friends. She reached them, however, but not to greet them. Her father and two weeping sisters, with others, stood around what all supposed to be her dying bed.

Dr. Newton had been informed of her case; and, in the unbounded kindness of his heart (contrary to his practice), he left his house, and hastened to the sick girl.

The solemnity and impressiveness of that scene will for ever be remembered by all who were present, but it can never be described. In a manner (as the doctor truly says) peculiar to himself, he treated the unconscious and apparently dying patient; and in less than three minutes she sat up in bed. She then arose to her feet, and walked the floor with the doctor's assistance.

Her pain and suffering had all gone. Her spine, which had not been touched for years without giving her intense pain, could now be roughly handled by all present. Food was immediately ordered; and amid the solemn silence of the room, where there was no sound save the sobs and fast-flowing tears of joy, she partook of the food. She ate heartily, and relished and enjoyed such a meal as she had not done in five years.

I am forced to look back with wonder and amazement at the above-described scene, and bound to acknowledge that it is beyond the reach of my mind to understand. I have only to say that her pleasant voice and cheerful smile greet us at the table of the family circle daily: she has continued to improve from that hour, and stands to-day a living witness, ever ready to testify to the power and goodness of her heavenly Father, as extended to her through the kind-hearted and benevolent Dr. Newton.

MOSES CRISTY,
No. 380, Pearl Street, New York.

As we spoke of seeing blindness cured. we will give one affidavit.

Peter Manning, being sworn, deposes and says: I live in Bordentown, N.J. On the 30th of October, 1862, I called on Dr. J. R. Newton. I was blind two years and three months. When I came to Dr. Newton, I was so bad that I could not see a gaslight in front of me; after ten minutes' treatment, without pain, I was enabled to see to read and write, and have kept my own books ever since. PETER MANNING.

Sworn and subscribed before me, this fourth day of March, 1863. WM. P. HIBBERD, *Alderman.*

Hundreds of testimonials such as the above could be gathered; but it is unnecessary. These cases are of such frequent occurrence, that the reader can very easily supply himself with all the documentary evidence necessary.

Now, in all candor, permit us to ask, What can be done with such cases as the above? They are before the world, and demand an explanation. Jesus said, "These signs shall follow them that believe." Are they not sufficient to prove, to those who think, that there are true believers, at least, among the Spiritualists? A conversation once occurred between ourself and a lady of the Advent faith, which sufficiently illustrates the point: —

LADY. — "I saw you operate on Mrs. —— last evening; and, though we supposed her case to be hopeless, she was perfectly restored in a few minutes: but it was the Devil that cured her."

HULL. — "Pretty fine old gentleman, that Devil of yours. If that is a specimen of his character, he has been grossly slandered: what a pity that churches and ministers misrepresent everybody, not excepting even the Devil himself!"

L. — "The Devil is not so good, after all. He made Mrs. —— sick, and then sent you, his agent, to cure her."

H. — "Then Satan's kingdom is divided against itself, and can not stand: so we can begin to hope to soon get rid of his Majesty."

L. — "Not at all. They are all parts of the same work. The Devil made Mrs. —— sick, and then sent you, his agent, to make her well: he knew that she would see the *benevolence* manifested in curing her, rather than the *malevolence* of making her sick. He is removing disease from the lady for the sake of getting possession of her soul."

H. — "In your remarks you have given me another evidence that I am a disciple of Jesus; for he said, —

"'It is enough for the disciple that he be as his master, and the servant as his lord. If they have called the master of the house Beelzebub, how much more shall they call them of his household?' — Matt. x. 25.

"If such charges were brought by the popular church against a former healer, what better could we expect now?"

L. — "But *his* mission was divine: yours is not."

H. — "Spiritualists prove the divinity of their mission in the same way that Jesus proved his was an errand of mercy to humanity. If you will turn to Matt. xi. 2–6, you will read, —

"'Now, when John had heard in the prison the works of Christ, he sent two of his disciples, and said unto him, Art thou he that should come, or do we look for another? Jesus answered and said unto them, Go and show John again those things which ye do hear and see: the blind receive their sight, and the lame walk, the lepers are cleansed, and the deaf hear, the dead are raised up, and the poor have the gospel preached unto them.'

"Now, I ask, in all candor, Was Jesus' logic good? Did he prove the divinity of his mission by such works? Then will not the same works prove the divinity of the power by which they are wrought? How startling your logic! you prove Jesus a God by his good works, and healing-mediums Devils by the same!"

L. — "I do not choose to argue with you. Christ is coming shortly to destroy the works of the Devil: then these questions will be settled."

H. — "Christ came once in the person of Jesus of Nazareth, and through him did many great works; but he was, according to promise, to come again, not in the person of *one* reformer. Jude says, —

"'Behold he cometh with ten thousand of his saints.' — Verse 14.

"The Greek word rendered 'with,' in this text, is *en*, and should be rendered 'in.' The Christ-power came once in one reformer; now it has come in *ten thousand* mediums: so that almost every hamlet on the continent has the evidence that the second coming of the Christ is accomplishing more than was accomplished through the mediumship of Jesus."

L. — "But where are the clouds? He was to come in the clouds."

H. — "So he was to come on horseback. John says, —

"'And I saw heaven opened, and, behold, a white horse; and he that sat upon him was called Faithful and True; and in righteousness he doth judge and make war. His eyes were a flame of fire, and on his head were many crowns; and he had a name written, that no man knew but he himself. And he was clothed in a vesture dipped in blood; and his name is called, The Word of God. And the armies which were in heaven followed him upon white horses, clothed in fine linen, white and clean. And out of his mouth goeth a sharp sword, that with it he should smite the nations; and he shall rule them with a rod of iron; and he treadeth the wine-press of the fierceness and wrath of Almighty God. And he hath on his vesture and on his thigh a name written, KING OF KINGS, AND LORD OF LORDS.' — Rev. xix. 11–16.

"But who looks for 'the King of kings and Lord of lords' on an old gray horse, because of this declaration? May not the clouds, like the horses, be symbols? Clouds of witnesses are mentioned in the Bible; and to-day it is said that there are *eleven millions* of witnesses of the living Christ-power manifested on earth at the present time. I tell you Christ is here: you have had a demonstration of it in the healing of this lady."

L. — "But the grave is to yield up its victory, and death its sting, when Christ comes: I do not see as that is done."

H. — "I do. Once I regarded death as a dark and

cruel foe. When my friends were taken from me, if they were not stung, I was. Now the grave into which I used to look for my mother holds her no longer. *I know she is not there.* I have seen her and talked with her. She lives to-day; and, for myself, death has lost its sting. I do not dread it. It is natural; it is right: but I never could see it so until it was manifest in the second coming of Christ."

This chapter has already grown beyond the limits intended; but we can not conclude without issuing a challenge to the theological world. Not for words, but *deeds.* We call for a convention of the religious world, the object of which shall be to ascertain where the true believers are, the matter to be tested by their works. Jesus says the believers shall accomplish even greater works than were wrought through his mediumship. Are the churches believers? Will they try it? If they will go into convention, and do the works Jesus did, we propose, in behalf of Spiritualism, to acknowledge them believers. If they can not, will they be honest enough to confess themselves infidels? After they have all tried and failed, as fail they will as sure as they try, we are willing to be one of twenty mediums (that is one hundred less in number than they had on the day of Pentecost), who will go upon the same rostrum, into the same assembly where the churches failed; and if we do not, in a less space of time than ten days, accomplish all that was done by the disciples within the first ten days after the ascension of Jesus, we will acknowledge that Spiritualists are like the churches, — they are infidels. If, however, we accomplish the work, will the orthodox world take back the slanderous, libelous charge of infidelity? We hand out this challenge in all sincerity, yet not with any hope that it will be accepted.

That all strife and sectism may give place to the pure doctrines and practices which make men better, and prove them humble followers after all truth and virtue, is our most earnest prayer.

CHAPTER VII.

ARE WE DELUDED?

A Common Cry — Contradictory Positions — Order of Batteries — They fire into each other — "Kettle Story" — Result of the Warfare — Dialogue — God and Mediums deceiving the World — Are God and the Devil Partners — Is it just to damn the World for Unbelief — Author loves God more than Bibles — Lying Spirits sent out — Did God do it — Case of Jeremiah and Ezekiel — Ezekiel's Explanation — Spiritualism a Delusion — The Lord coming — Reasoning in a Circle — Wonderful Success of the Opposition (?) — Spiritualism will not "down" — "Old Split-foot" — Toe-joint Theory — Hidden Meaning in appointing these Committees — The Machinery Argument — Arguments of Opposers suicidal to themselves — Human Testimony rejected — Conditions required — Conditions of Sleep — Conversation with a Photographist — Conditions of Photography — Telegraphy — Arguments against Spiritualism would overthrow the Bible — An Infidel Deacon denies his Bible — A Giant Delusion — Spiritualism Twenty-two Years ago and now — A prospective View — Spiritualism Positive and Aggressive — Reasons for going to Church — Churches not Proselyting — Why do Persons become Spiritualists — Rev. A. J. Frishback's Reply — Suffering for Spiritualism — Ministers' Wives in the Lunatic Asylum for Spiritualism — Author's Experience — The Quality of Converts to Spiritualism — Our Evidence not in the Number or Intelligence of Converts — Giant Minds yield — Atheism and Materialism give Place — Hon. N. P. Talmadge and J. W. Edmonds — "The Kings of the Earth" — Opposers fall before the Power — Gamaliel's Opinion — A charming Delusion — Efforts to convert a Spiritualist — Death-bed Scene — "Oh, happy Delusion!" — It is not a Delusion — Child Medium.

FOR more than a score of years the opponents of Spiritualism have been following it with the cry of "*delusion!*" The only thing our opponents have ever been able to agree in, is, that Spiritualism is some kind of a delusion. Notwithstanding all agree so far, it excites the mirthfulness of a Spiritualist who is posted up as to its evidences to hear the various contradictory positions taken by those whose bread and butter depends upon putting it down. Indeed, we ought not to laugh at their calamity; for if their *lives*, instead of their *living*, depended on writing and preaching Spiritualism down, they could not succeed any better.

Not long since, it was our privilege to attend a discussion where five men affirmed that Spiritualism was a delusion. They succeeded admirably in agreeing so far: but here the agreement ended; for, before they had finished their arguments, they had taken every one of the nine contradictory positions usually brought to bear against it and each other. Each speaker succeeded in placing himself on as many sides of each of the contradictory positions usually brought to bear against each other as his limited time would allow. As we listened to the logic of these *killers* of Spiritualism, we thought, What a wonder it does not die, men shooting at it from *nine* different directions! There are only two reasons why opponents have failed to kill Spiritualism: one is, they have ever fired more shots at each other than at their common enemy; the other is, Spiritualism is "iron-clad." Bunker-Hill Monument could be battered down with popguns easier than the monument erected by the angel-world to show its existence, power, and victories, could be overthrown by the artillery of infidel church-members.

If the batteries pelting at Spiritualism were named and numbered, they would be about as follows: —

Battery No. 1. — "And for this cause God shall send them strong delusion, that they should believe a lie; that they all might be damned who believed not the truth, but had pleasure in unrighteousness." — 2 Thess. ii. 11, 12.

"Spiritualism is God's delusion."

Battery No. 2. — "Even him whose coming is after the working of Satan, with all power and signs and lying wonders, and with all deceivableness of unrighteousness in them that perish; because they received not the love of the truth, that they might be saved." — 2 Thess. ii. 9, 10.

"For they are the spirits of devils, working miracles, which go forth unto the kings of the earth and of the whole world, to gather them to the battle of that great day of God Almighty." — Rev. xvi. 11.

"Spiritualism is Satan's last and greatest delusion."

Battery No. 3. — "The manifestations are produced by machinery."

Battery No. 4. — "They are all wicked spirits."

Battery No. 5. — "It is electricity."

Battery No. 6. — "There are no manifestations. Spiritualists are for the most part idiotic or insane. Those who are not are lying knaves, dealing out deceptions to the credulous."

Battery No. 7. — "Spiritualism is a contagious disease, working on the mind as small-pox or cholera does on the body."

Battery No. 8. — "God anciently made laws against it: it is therefore wicked to have any thing to do with it."

Battery No. 9. — "It is new: we should inquire for the old paths, and stick to the religion of our fathers."

One would naturally think, that, under the fires of *nine* as formidable guns as these look to be, Spiritualism would be compelled to surrender; but, when the smoke and fog occasioned by this contest clears away, we assure all that not a shell has entered the *arena* of Spiritualism. God-delusions and Devil-delusions have been shooting at each other, and both are the worse for the battle. The machinery and wicked-spirit arguments have, after pitching into all the other theories, fallen from blows received from each other. The electricity and juggler theories have annihilated each other. The last-mentioned battery — that it is *new* and therefore untrue — has, after silencing the battery stationed where God anciently made laws against Spiritualism, surrendered to fires from eight directions.

Really such a jumble of absurdities reminds us of the "lawyer's kettle." A noted member of the bar, in summing up the evidence in defense of a client who had borrowed a kettle and returned it broken, said, "May it please the Court, we have proved, first, that the kettle was broken when we borrowed it; second, that it was whole when we took it home; and, third, that we never had the old kettle anyhow."

The answer to the most of these objections must be reserved for another chapter. We only design here to note the consistency, or rather inconsistency, of opponents. This bushwhacking mode of warfare has resulted, as might have been expected, in converting people to Spiritualism by the million, until now the number of Spiritualists can not be computed; even our opponents, some of them, setting it as high as *eleven millions.* Were there eleven millions of Spiritualists two years since, when this computation was made? If so, they were eleven millions of evidences that the batteries erected against Spiritualism have slain that many more in their own ranks than in ours.

Once, in traveling through the Western States, we fell into the company of a minister who was perfectly sure that Spiritualism was a delusion. The substance of what passed between us may be embodied in the following dialogue: —

MINISTER. — "I have not a doubt but that Spiritualism is the delusion spoken of in 2 Thess. ii. 11."

HULL. — "Then Spiritualists are God's servants, and you are fighting against him."

MIN. — "No. How can that be?"

H. — "The text asserts that 'God shall send them strong delusions.' If your interpretation is correct, *God has sent several thousand mediums into the world*, with *a delusion to deceive the world;* and they would accomplish it, if it were not that *you are exposing the plans of God and the mediums.*"

MIN. — "God has nothing to do with it; he is opposed to it: it is Satan who is working, with power, signs, and lying wonders."

H. — "Your first text said it was God who was after the people with a delusion: now you have quoted another verse of the same chapter to prove that it is the Devil. Must I understand that the Devil is God's agent, — that he is working among the people because God sends them a delusion? or is God and the Devil each after them with a deception called Spiritualism?"

MIN. — "There is the text: make of it what you can. God will damn the world for unbelief; and Spiritualists have departed from the faith, and denied every cardinal doctrine of the Bible."

H. — "And so you are going to have the world damned for unbelief, are you?"

MIN. — "I am not: God is."

H. — "Is there any justice in that? Do I make

my own faith or want of faith? Can I govern my own belief more than I can the color of my eyes or hair? Is not God my Author? and is he not the Author of truth? If I fail to harmonize with truth, am I, who neither made my common sense, nor yet the stories I can not believe, to blame? But your text asserts more than that. It does not simply say that God will punish unbelief; but it declares that God will send strong delusion after them, *that they may believe a lie*, that he may damn them. I say this is unjust."

MIN. — "If you loved your Bible, you would not dare to speak as you do."

H. — "I love my Bible, and believe more of it each day than I did the day previous; but, dearly as I love the Bible, I love God more. I could not see his *character* sacrificed in this manner for any book. I find it much easier to believe Paul could be a little mistaken in an hypothesis, than to think God stoops thus to deceive his own children."

MIN. — "You should not reject the Bible because of an isolated expression like that. There are spots on the sun."

H. — "Though I by no means reject the Bible, I assure you this is not an isolated expression. If you will turn to 1 Kings, xxii. 19–23, you will read, —

"'And he said, Hear thou therefore the word of the Lord: I saw the Lord sitting on his throne, and all the host of heaven standing by him, on his right hand and on his left. And the Lord said, Who shall persuade Ahab, that he may go up and fall at Ramoth-gilead? And one said on this manner, and another said on that manner. And there came forth a spirit, and stood before the Lord, and said, I will persuade him. And the Lord said unto him, Wherewith? And he said, I will go forth, and I will be a lying spirit in the mouth of all his prophets. And he said, Thou shalt persuade him, and prevail also: go forth and do so. Now, therefore, behold, the Lord hath put a lying spirit in the mouth of all these thy prophets, and the Lord hath spoken evil concerning thee.'

"Now, there is a sense in which I believe this paragraph, and a sense in which I do not. If you ask me if I believe God sent a lying spirit, I answer, No. If I believe a lying spirit operated on all the prophets, including Micaiah, I say, Yes. But God does not stoop thus to conquer. Those disembodied wags who influenced the prophets perhaps thought their predictions were correct, and knew they would have more weight upon a self-conceited, ignorant king if they professed to come from Almighty God. You will remember, there were four hundred of these, all bearing testimony the same way, except Micaiah, who crossed his own track. Now let me ask, Do you believe God did it? Is it not more charitable, to say the least, to believe the Bible writer correct as to fact, and mistaken as to hypothesis?"

MIN. — "These prophets were false prophets: no true prophet was ever led astray in that way."

H. — "There is no evidence that these prophets were any more false than all the others. Jeremiah and Ezekiel were each deceived in the same way. Jeremiah says, —

"'O Lord, thou hast deceived me, and I was deceived: thou art stronger than I, and hast prevailed: I am in derision daily, every one mocketh me.' — Jer. xx. 7.

"Now, I frankly acknowledge I do not believe that text; but do not misunderstand me. I grant that Jeremiah was deceived; yes, deceived by lying spirits: but, when he accuses the Ruler of the Universe of deceiving him, I think he was mistaken. Again I say, 'Let God be true, though it make every man a liar.' As to Ezekiel, though he was one of the best physical and clairvoyant mediums in the world, he never uttered a truth in any of his predictions. His prophecies, more than all others, were the cause of a proverb to which he refers as follows: —

"'And the word of the Lord came unto me, saying, Son of man, what is that proverb that ye have in the land of Israel, saying, The days are prolonged, and every vision faileth? Tell them, therefore, Thus saith the Lord God: I will make this proverb to cease, and they shall no more use it as a proverb in Israel; but say unto them, The days are at hand, and the effect of every vision. For there shall be no more any vain vision nor flattering divination within the house of Israel. For I am the Lord: I will speak, and the word that I shall speak shall come to pass; it shall be no more prolonged: for in your days, O rebellious house, will I say the word, and will perform it, saith the Lord God. Again the word of the Lord came to me, saying, Son of man, behold, they of the house of Israel say, The vision that he seeth is for many days to come, and he prophesieth of the times that are far off. Therefore say unto them, Thus saith the Lord God: There shall none of my words be prolonged any more; but the word which I have spoken shall be done, saith the Lord God.' — Ezek. xii. 21–28.

"Here the spirit acknowledges the truth of the proverb, but says he will make it to cease; that is, there shall be no more any vain visions, nor any prophecies which applied to the distant future, but the effect of every vision is at hand. Again Ezekiel accounts for his false visions and prophecies as follows: —

"'And if the prophet be deceived when he hath spoken a thing, I the Lord have deceived that prophet; and I will stretch out my hand upon him, and will destroy him from the midst of my people Israel.' — Ezek. xiv. 9.

"Once more I will confess, I do not believe the Lord deceives. I find it easier to believe Ezekiel was a little mistaken in supposing that influence came from 'the Father of Lights with whom there is no variableness, neither shadow of turning.'"

Min. — "Aren't you off the track? We commenced to talk about Spiritualism, and you have gone off into a tirade of abuse of the Bible. Why do you not stick to the question?"

H. — "I have not abused the Bible, only your interpretation of certain portions of it; but I will hear what you have to say about Spiritualism."

Min. — "I say, and can prove, that Spiritualism is the delusion spoken of by Paul."

H. — "How do you prove it? You know there never has been a religious theory which has dared to drive out of the beaten track, but that this text has been quoted to prove it a delusion."

Min. — "I prove my point thus: This delusion is to come up in the *last days*. The Lord's coming is after the working of Satan with power, signs, and lying wonders. Signs are so ominous that there is no room left for doubt. The coming of the Lord is right upon us; but we look for the Devil's work, — the great delusion, — and find Spiritualism, and that alone, coming at the right time, and answering the other specifications of the prophecy. We are, therefore, justified in the conclusion that Spiritualism is the delusion."

H. — "That would do if you could prove your major proposition, that the coming of the Lord is near."

MIN. — "That is easily proved; for, when Spiritualism comes up, the coming of the Lord follows immediately after."

Here the call of "Change cars for Madison!" terminated our conversation. We wanted to dissect our friend's logic for him, but had not the time. The logic comes in thus: —

Proposition No. 1. — "The Lord is coming."

Conclusion No. 1. — "Therefore Spiritualism is a delusion."

Prop. No. 2. — "Spiritualism is a delusion."

Con. No. 2. — "Therefore the Lord is coming."

What accommodating logic! The conclusion of the first proposition forms a basis for the second; and that of the second quite as accommodatingly "wheels into line," and forms a basis for the first. If this is not a fair specimen of what logicians call "reasoning in a circle," we acknowledge we never saw one.

We now come to the direct question: Is Spiritualism a delusion? A brief examination of its history will answer the question. If the arguments of the opposers of Spiritualism be true, then verily is "truth stranger than fiction." Its statement would be about as follows:

Twenty-one years ago, two little girls, members of a respectable family, one of them *nine* and the other *eleven* years old, undertook, without any motive whatever, to delude and deceive the world. We say without motive; for certainly there was no money in the deception, and there could not possibly have been any honor gained by it. These youths would have succeeded, had it not been that the ministers, doctors, and some of the lawyers, organized a warfare against them, in which their talents, books and learning were brought into such effectual operation that, at the end of nineteen years, according to figures made by those making the attack, the children had only succeeded in making about eleven millions of converts!

"A stitch in time saves nine." Perhaps the reason of the success (?) of the opposition was their early, unrelenting, and untiring warfare. For the battle was commenced before a test was given. It is also an acknowledged axiom, that "in union there is strength." The opposition was certainly united in one position, if no more; that is, Spiritualism must be put down at whatever cost. They paid the cost, "'quitted themselves like men," sacrificed all, in many cases not excepting their honor; but Spiritualism proved to be a "Banquo's ghost:" it would not "down."

Before any intelligence had been derived from the mysterious noises, we remember to have heard it suggested that it was the Devil. Indeed, that charge was so common, that, long before they learned there was any intelligence connected with it, the little girls used to address it as "Old Split-foot." By an accident it was ascertained that this power was intelligent, could answer questions, and give other signs of knowing what was said to it.

As soon as a communication was received containing an undeniable test, committees were appointed to investigate and put it down. The first committee very readily and learnedly came to two conclusions: The first was, Spiritualism is a delusion. The second related to the *modus operandi* of that deception. The world was informed that the facts were simply these: The little girls, in going to school, got their toes frozen. When that was ascertained, the mother wet some linen in turpentine, and wrapped the toes in it: there was a connection between the toe-joint, the linen, and the turpentine, that produced the concussions. This expose of the delusion did not last very long. The opposers had too many toes, and there was too much turpentine and linen among them. With all these implements for producing manifestations, they failed to produce one single rap.

This made it necessary to appoint another committee; and here, permit us to say, there is a world of meaning in the appointment of this and other committees. It means, first, there are phenomena there which demand investigation; second, other committees, learned men as they were, failed to give us a proper solution of these manifestations.

Other committees soon came to several conclusions: the first always was, that Spiritualism was a delusion; and the second generally was, that all previous committees were deluded. The knee-joint theory, machinery theory, and all other systems of opposition to Spiritualism, had their day. Spiritualism lived to bury them all. "There is machinery in the table," was the cry raised by Prof. Matteson, and hundreds of others who would have been professors, but lacked the ability to cope with this learned blackguard. Many attended circles on purpose to detect the machinery, when, lo! the raps were heard not only on the tables, but on chairs, stoves, stove-pipes, the walls of the house, the floor, the ceiling, and even sometimes on the hands, feet, heads, and teeth of sitters. Thus the warfare went on; the world *exposing* its folly in attempting to expose Spiritualism, and the angel-world daily handing out new demonstrations of power.

There is a proverb, that "the gods first make mad those whom they would destroy." In this case, it is literally true; for there has never yet been an argument adduced against Spiritualism, but that weighs with all of its force against the religion, science, or profession of the one making the argument. The mocking priests demanded that Jesus should come down from the cross, and they would believe; but he could not come down to satisfy a scoffing mob: so priests now, often with as much audacity and little sense, throw themselves back on their dignity, and demand the production of manifestations impossible under the circumstances. One of these specimens of the *genus homo*, in a discussion with us, positively forbade the introduction of human testimony. Human beings were liable to be deceived, and some would lie; so he would not take even *sworn* testimony that tables had been seen to move, concussions heard, and pencils seen to write without any visible agency. Nothing would do but the production of such phenomena in that audience, at that time. Our reply was, that certain conditions were necessary, which could not obtain in a promiscuous assembly; that any person proposing to do any thing had a right to state the conditions upon which he could do the thing, and no one had a right to demand the production of the phenomena until all the conditions had been obeyed. "If it can be done anywhere, it can be done here," was his reply; "and now is the time. We do not care what has been done elsewhere: produce your manifestations here, and we will believe."

To illustrate the absurdity of his position, suppose sleep to be the phenomenon in question. A hundred witnesses swearing that they had slept, and seen others sleep, would not convince him: he would demand of the one who affirmed that one-third of every healthy person's time is spent in sleep, that he should lie down on the rostrum, and go to sleep in the presence of the audience to convince him. Is there one who reads this book who could do it? We think not. The conditions of sleep do not obtain under such circumstances. The fact of trying to go to sleep as a test would keep one awake if he had not slept in six months. The light in the room, the magnetism of the audience, and all other conditions, would go to prevent sleep. Any one can sleep better in the dark than in well-lighted apartments. Now, if the opposers will learn that conditions for good spirit-manifestations are required to be quite as negative as for sleep, they will cease to exhibit so much folly in their opposition. There is not an opposer of Spiritualism in the world to-day, who does not require conditions for certain manifestations in his daily business that he obstinately refuses to give to the spirit-world.

The following incident faithfully illustrates the absurd position taken by a majority of opposers. We were invited by a friend, a photographist, to go to his gallery, and sit for a picture. We had hardly entered the room, when our friend, in a good-natured way, commenced a tirade against Spiritualism. A dark circle he would not sit in under any circumstances; and, as to other conditions, they were only an excuse behind which to hide fraud, deception, and falsehood. "In fact," said he, "I get mad every time I hear the word 'conditions.'" — "And yet," said I, "you require conditions every time you take a photograph. I can take a better likeness with my printing-press than you can with your *camera*, if you will permit me first to destroy your conditions. You first require the subject to sit passive and quiet. He must be willing you should take a picture; your *camera* must be properly adjusted; you require just such an amount of light; and it must come from the right direction. Then, by having your chemicals prepared with mathematical precision, and your plates just right, you can do part of your work; yet you are compelled to go into the dark before you can develop a picture.

"Now understand one thing: the chemicals spirits use in coming in communion with earth are as much finer than those used by yourself as heaven is higher than earth. You, who require such implicit yielding to such subtile conditions, are the last one who should fall out with that word, or object to the idea it contains. Now, you ask mediums to go into a hall, and on the rostrum produce certain kinds of spirit-manifestation: they will do it when you go to the same hall, on to the same rostrum, and, under the same circumstances, produce genuine and good photographic likenesses."

Thus it is: the man could not see until shown by this illustration that his argument weighed quite as heavily against his own occupation as against Spiritualism.

The man who enters the telegraph-office, tears the batteries from it, cuts the wires, and then demands from the operator communications from distant cities, is quite as sensible as those, who, after destroying all the conditions of spirit-manifestation, tauntingly demand spiritual phenomena. How much better to humbly sit in the quiet, and receive influxes from "over the river"!

We repeat, the Bible itself can not stand under the argument which kills Spiritualism. The whole Bible, with its stories a hundred times as large as any told by Spiritualists, is received on human hearsay testimony; and yet *living witnesses*, who can be questioned and cross-questioned, are disbelieved.

We were once, at a dinner-party, introduced to a deacon. Soon the conversation turned upon Spiritualism. Having just read the debate between Prof. Leo Miller and Prof. J. Stanley Grimes, we decided to borrow one of Mr. Miller's bomb-shells. After relating several incidents known to persons present, all of which were stanchly denied by the deacon, — for he felt that the life of his religion hung upon his zeal in disputing every thing he himself had not witnessed, — at length we addressed ourself to Bro. R. (who was sitting by our side), as though we wanted no one else to hear, yet determined that all at the table should hear. "I read the history of a very strange manifestation this morning, which, if it proves true, ought to set men to thinking," said we. "Ah! what is it?" said R. "It happened in the old country," we replied. "A man was sick, and sent for a healing medium. Though he was not very sick, he thought he was going to die; and so the medium thought at first. Soon, however, he obtained a communication, stating that he would recover; whereupon the man demanded a *sign*. Well, said the medium, as an evidence that you shall get well, logs of wood, stones, and heaps of earth, shall move without any visible agency. And the document adds that these things did move, — that stones, and heaps of earth, of many tons' burthen, moved, to all appearance, of their own accord; and the man got well." We had hardly got through with our story, when our deacon asked, "Where did you say that happened?"—"In the old country," we responded. "I would like to see the papers for that," ejaculated the deacon: "I know it never occurred. If such things can be done anywhere, why not here? why locate them so far from home? No one but an insane person could swallow such a story."

We permitted him to blow until his ammunition was spent, and then coolly responded, "Deacon, if you will turn to 2 Kings xx., you will find the story. Hezekiah was the sick man; Isaiah was the medium; and the whole earth moved backward ten degrees to convince a man that a boil would not kill him. Now do you believe the story?" His only response was, "It is unfair to catch a man on a pin-hook." It may be unfair; but we have to do just such work occasionally. It serves to illustrate the admixture of credulity and incredulity in the religions of the day.

We now affirm, that, if modern Spiritualism is a delusion, it is a *giant* delusion. Not only has it utterly baffled the skill of opposers, whose cry has been, "Away with it!" "Let it be crucified!" but who can take a retrospective view of its work without an inexpressible degree of surprise? Twenty-two years ago, it was nothing, — not a book except the Bible written in its behalf, and that was regarded more as a dead letter than any thing else; not a press to advocate its claims; not a lecturer in the field; not a medium in the country; not a believer in the world. At that time one figure, and that a cipher, told all there was of Spiritualism. Not a quarter of a century since, it commenced amid the most determined opposition, has waded through it, and marched steadily on, until now its mediums are counted by thousands, and it would require a column and a half of "The New-York Ledger," set in *agate* type, to hold the names and post-office addresses of its public lecturers. Its weekly and monthly periodicals, scattered like autumn leaves, are read with more enthusiasm and delight than ever before. New volumes are continually being issued from its presses; its literature is being written and translated into foreign languages; and thus it spreads with a rapidity unequaled by any religion ever known before.

Now, considering the machinery already in running order for spreading Spiritualism, — its local, county, state, and national associations; the mediums and talent already in its ranks; and the number of living witnesses there are to its truths, — where will it be on the day of its fiftieth anniversary? *Where won't it be?* Another question: Where will its opposers be at that time? They will be where Pharaoh's "fat kine" were, after coming in contact with "the seven lean kine."

Modern Spiritualism, though born in a manger not twenty-five years since, is now the only *positive* religion in the world. All other religious theories live upon their negative elements. Ask almost any member of a popular church why he belongs where he does; and, if you get a true answer, it will be about as follows: "Oh! I must have somewhere to go: I have nothing to do, and there is no other place of amusement for me to attend on Sunday; and so I go to church. Why should I not? My father and mother always did the same thing; my friends and associates go there; we have good music, and a smart preacher, who preaches smooth things to fashionable ears: in fact, the current sets that way, and I drift with it." Another goes to be in fashion; another to exhibit fine clothing; another to get the custom of some one who attends; another to see how church-people dress, hear who is married, who is dead; and so forth, to the end of the chapter.

Ask again, "What were you before you were a Methodist, Baptist, or Presbyterian?" and you will probably be answered, "Why, I wasn't any thing: I never belonged to any other church or party." If you find one of a thousand who has left one religious church, and joined another, he has, as a general thing, done it without any change of faith or opinion. Some local disturbance or jealousy has been the cause of the change. Not more than half of those who belong to the church to-day know what the peculiar tenets of their church are; and six out of eight who do can not give a rational reason for their belief.

Now, go out among the Spiritualists, whose millions of converts have come from atheists, infidels, and *every church* in *Christendom*, and ask any one of them why he or she is a Spiritualist, and you will be pointed to some peculiar test, or some beautiful clause of our philosophy which arrested their attention, led them to a further investigation, and finally *forced* them out of their church. One said to us, "When my spirit-mother came and talked with me, and when I had learned that my wife, whom I regarded as dead, was still alive, my religion, my church, my friends, my popularity, and my prejudices were not all strong enough to hold me."

When Rev. A. J. Frishback turned his back on his church and salary, to preach these heaven-born truths, he was asked why he did it? His reply was, "I have seen the angels." Glorious privilege! Is it not enough to requite all our toil?

Ministers have left large congregations and fat salaries to become fellow-servants with angels. Lawyers have renounced their profession for the sake of these heaven-born truths. Husbands have been compelled to leave their wives, and wives their husbands, children have been turned away from their own homes, and parents forsaken in their old age, for their communion with those on the other side. Students, filled with all the ardor and vigor of youth, with the most flattering prospects ahead of them, have been driven from their colleges in disgrace, because of their allegiance to these higher powers.

Thus Spiritualism proves itself a positive philosophy, enabling those who embrace it to forsake all, and stem the flood of opposition, for its truths. The author of these pages is personally acquainted with two ladies, one of them the wife of a Presbyterian minister, who were by their husbands driven to the alternative of renouncing their Spiritualism or going to the lunatic asylum. They both, though more sane than their husbands and church-going neighbors, chose the latter, preferring a life of imprisonment among the insane, rather than one of ease and luxury based on their want of fidelity to their risen friends and the God who spake in their own souls..

The flames of slander, calumny, and persecution through which we have passed in consequence of our having turned from a former belief, the poverty we have endured because of our allegiance to our friends on the other side, could not have been borne, had it not been for the *living* evidence which almost hourly came to us, of the truth and divinity of our cause. That, together with the angelic forces backing us up, would enable us to "run through a troop or leap over a wall."

> "A scrip on my back,
> And a staff in my hand,
> I march on in haste
> Through an enemy's land:
> The road may be rough,
> But it can not be long;
> I'll smooth it with hope
> And I'll cheer it with song."

A word on the *quality* of the converts to Spiritualism might not be amiss, although the argument drawn from *quantity* or *quality* is not relied upon to prove it true. The evidence of its truth to us is the same whether there were another believer in the world or not. Nor does our faith hang on the intelligence of those who believe, but upon a combination of biblical and modern facts with a philosophy which adapts itself to the wants of the human soul: so with every Spiritualist. The number and intelligence of those slain by its power only proves to us that facts which we perceive are universally adapting themselves to the intelligent everywhere.

The myriads who have flocked around the standard of Spiritualism have, in many instances, been men and women of giant intellect. It will not be disputed that Robert Hare, Robert Owen, Hon. Robert Dale Owen, Hon. Joshua R. Giddings, Hon. N. P. Talmadge, Hon. J. W. Edmonds, Hon. B. F. Wade, and Wm. Lloyd Garrison, are men of brains. They are among those slain by its power.

Robert Hare, Robert Owen, and Robert Dale Owen, were thoroughly posted with regard to all the theologies as well as the literature of the age. They were known the world over to be stanch and rigid atheists. They had withstood the batteries of all the pulpits in the land; and bundles upon bundles of quills were used up in trying to write their atheism down: but all to no purpose. Robert Owen had put to flight all the ministers in the land; but he, as well as his son, and Prof. Hare of the Smithsonian Institute, was at last compelled to yield to spirit-voices. Two of these sires are traveling on in the sunshine of the spirit-world, while the other is filling places of trust in our own government, and writing and lecturing on Spiritualism.

N. P. Talmadge and Joshua R. Giddings have also left the Indian summer of this life, and gone to help form a battery in the brighter summer-land. While these "noble dead" are thus employed, Judge Edmonds is writing alternately on Spiritualism and Jurisprudence.

Were we to leave this country, and go to the Old World, we should find the Queen of England always having a place fixed at the table for her departed consort. She has not a doubt that he occupies the "vacant chair" which she causes to be provided for him. On the authority of "The New-York Sun," we can state that the Empress Eugénie attends circles every day; while it is well known that Louis Napoleon is a Spiritualist, even in person attending the circles held by the brothers Davenport, and giving them fine presents as tokens of his appreciation of the powers manifesting through them. Thus Spiritualism proves itself adapted alike to the king on his throne and the beggar in his hovel.

Still another argument on the power of Spiritualism might be based upon the fact of its opposers, one after another, laying down the weapons of warfare, and finally, many of them, taking up their line of march with it. The weaker and less strategetic power in every battle must yield to the stronger. The test of strength in the powers engaged in this warfare can be told in the fact that there are few able advocates of Spiritualism to-day, who did not graduate in the field of opposition. Prof. Leo Miller used all his talents and education, and spent several of the last years of his life, in assailing Spiritualism. E. V. Wilson was told by spirits who appeared to him as Jesus did to Paul, that he must ground the weapons of his rebellion. Dr. P. B. Randolph got tired of the warfare, and concluded he would sail with the popular current. He tried to write and preach Spiritualism into its grave; but "found it hard to kick against the pricks." His efforts recoiled on his own head: he was compelled to return to the religion he so grossly slandered. Dr. J. B. Dodd wrote a book against Spiritualism; but the printer's ink had scarcely dried on it, when he had renounced it, and declared himself a Spiritualist. We ourself went into a twelve-years' crusade against Spiritualism (those who read our writings, and listened to our sermons and debates, can judge with what amount of ability); but, like others, we were compelled to surrender. D. W. Hull, our brother "after the flesh," after spending six years in preparation to whip our Spiritualism out of us, whipped himself into it, and has become an eyesore to all opposers. Thus it is: the "Sauls of Tarsus" are permitted to carry the warfare just so far, when, lo! they find themselves smitten with blindness from the spirit-world.

With all these facts staring us in the face, who can doubt that Spiritualism, whether true or false, is a giant well worthy the steel of Orthodox ministers and Harvard professors? No position, no learning, no religion, no power, has been a match for it. It has gone on from conquering to conquest. As we view its onward march, we are reminded of the language of Gamaliel of old to the opposers of ancient Spiritualism, —

"And now I say unto you, Refrain from these men, and let them alone: for, if this counsel or this work be of men, it will come to nought; but if it be of God, ye can not overthrow it, lest, haply, ye be found even to fight against God." — Acts v. 38, 39.

Spiritualism has indeed, if this test be taken, proved itself of God.

Though Spiritualism is a giant, it is not a huge, un-

14

comely *monster* to be dreaded. If a delusion at all, it is a *charming* delusion. On this division of the subject, it is needless to remark at length, as our first chapter is a sufficient elucidation of this department of the subject. We would only ask, Who would not enjoy the consolation of knowing that his friends whom the world calls dead still live? Where is the devoted wife who would not enjoy social intercourse with the companion recently departed from her embrace? Spiritualism has opened the eyes of many thousands to see the beyond; and myriads who once groped in darkness are now receiving messages of love and wisdom from the angel world. Is that delusion? Then let us live and die charmed with just such delusion!

In a Western city was a railroad-station agent, who was known, wherever known at all, as a Spiritualist. Persons of all grades of belief tried to persuade him to renounce his allegiance to his spirit-friends. They displayed before his view, in glowing colors, the transitory glories of earth, which he might enjoy if he would only say nothing of his offensive Spiritualism; but all to no purpose. He was finally told by a minister who could not resist the power of his honest logic, that such doctrine did very well to live by, but would not sustain a soul in the moment of dissolution. "If," said the reverend, "I could be present at your death-bed, I would see you wring your hands, and cry for mercy; then you would call for the consolations of the religion you now spurn for the effervescent bauble of Spiritualism."

Said the brother, "If you are in the city when I am called to exchange worlds, you shall see whether your words are true."

In a few days from that time, upon a cold and icy morning, when coupling the cars together, his feet slipped, and the cars passed over his thighs, severing his limbs from his body. When, in a few moments, he was informed that his earthly career was drawing to a close, and if he had any thing to say, now was his last chance, after appointing one to attend to his business, he sent for his friends who had urged him to renounce his acquaintance with the angels. When they were all assembled, he spoke to the minister substantially as follows: —

"You expressed a desire to see a Spiritualist die. My time has come: now you shall be gratified. I have believed Spiritualism, and rejoiced for the past ten years in its consolations. Now I know, as I never did before, that it is true. As the flesh grows weaker, the spirit gains strength. *I see the angels, I hear them sing: they are waiting for me.*"

After a moment's pause, he continued, —

"Some of my family belong to your church, and will want you to deliver my funeral-address. Will you promise to tell the audience that I was a Spiritualist, and died such; that Spiritualism afforded a consolation which sustained me in a dying hour?"

The minister promised, and kept his word. After the dying man obtained this promise, he seemed perfectly resigned. He talked of his hope while strength lasted. Finally, after lying motionless and speechless, with his eyes closed a few moments, he opened them, and gazed on his friends for a brief period. His eyes sparkling all the while with an unearthly luster, he said, "They are calling; I must go. Good-by!" And in a moment his spirit was borne into the country where disputes on such questions are settled.

Is this delusion? Then let us live and die deluded! If it is a delusion which has made us happier and better for the last six years of our life; if a delusion has sustained us amid trials and troubles, and enabled us each day to say, "Though I walk through the valley of the shadow of death, I will fear no evil," — then, welcome, delusion! May thy cords be lengthened, and thy stakes strengthened, until thy banners wave over the ruins of error and superstition, and every heart is made glad with a knowledge of angelic communion!

> "Whispers of Eden given
> Greet mine ear,
> As if nearer bringing heaven, —
> Still more near;
> Calling upward, sweetly calling
> To the sky,
> Wait, my weary soul to welcome
> By and by.
> Oh! how my longing soul will spring
> To rise and join them on the wing."

Now, we affirm that Spiritualism is not a delusion. On this, as on the last division of this subject, we will do but little more than to refer our readers to the foregoing pages of this volume. If the evidences already presented can be avoided, any amount of just such evidence is worthless.

If Samuel, Moses, Elijah, Jesus, and others returned in the ages gone, then they proved that the dead can return. If our friends who loved and visited us while in the flesh love us still, they will come to us with blessings. If the history of the one and twenty years last past is correct, they have, they do come.

We have received so many tests, in so many ways, under so many varying circumstances, — many of which preclude the possibility of deception, — that we can not doubt.

We know a little girl not yet four years old, who occasionally has the name of a departed friend come in raised letters on her arm. She is not old enough to think of deceiving, much less is she capable of deciphering the names of friends, or of writing them if she knew them. Such evidences are unmistakable proofs of a supermundane power.

CHAPTER VIII.

OBJECTIONS ANSWERED.

Objections usually the Result of Ignorance — A British Lord and the Steamboat — Objections to the Telegraph — Objections to Abolitionism — God legislated against Spiritualism — Necromancy; Definition of — The Objection proves Spiritualism — Hebrews inclined to apply to the Dead for Knowledge — Law indorsed Spiritualism — This Law abolished — Other Precepts of this Law not binding — Jesus violated this Law — Paul and John violated, and hence deserve Death — The Law good in its Place, and for its Time — Men inclined to worship Spirits which communicated — The Jewish Jehovah not an Infinite God — He incited the Jews to Crime — Jehovah jealous of other Spirits — God goes to Babel to find out concerning a Report — Moses a better Man than his God — Heathen Gods once Men upon Earth — Spirits should be Helps, not Masters — Jews worshiped Spirits; Abraham, Lot, Joshua, Peter, John — Law against Spiritualism had evil Results — Materialism the Results of that Law — Elihu a Clairvoyant Medium — Men not Clay — "Old Paths" — Contradictory Objections — Consistency a rare Jewel — All Things were once new — Protestantism once new — Catholic Argument against Protestantism — All Religions have run the same Gantlet — "Fanatical Methodists" — Novelty not against Truth — Men in this World are learning; may not others progress — Spiritualism not new — Martin Luther and the Spirits — Wesley and the Spirits — They are Devils — An old Charge — John the Baptist and Jesus had a Devil — Every Reform was instigated by the Devil — Devil left the Church — Devil is Synonymous with Hatred of Progress — The Telescope, Fanning-Mill, Printing-Press, and Vaccination, all of the Devil — Devil discovered the Circulation of the Blood — Devil and Michael Servetus — Martyrdom of Servetus — The Devil and Vaccination — The Devil figuring as an Abolitionist, Geologist, &c. — Has God sent a Scorpion for a Fish — What a God — The Existence of a Devil can not be reconciled with that of a good God — The Devil always proves himself right — Author of Progress — Devil a Myth — Conclusion.

WE believe it was Mr. Horn who said, "An objection can be stated in three lines, that it requires thirty pages to answer." Such is the fact. It is an easy matter to object to any thing; but when a position

BIN TRAVERLER FORM

Cut By: María Poleo #7 **Qty** 105 **Date** 08-26-26

Scanned By:____________________ **Qty**________ **Date**__________

Scanned Batch ID's

____________ ____________ ____________

Notes / Exceptions

____

is fairly proved, then to present objections shows more frequently the stupidity than the erudition of the objector. It requires no learning, logic, or tact to frame objections; while it often requires even more than *demonstration* to remove them. A British lord could prove that it was impossible for a boat to navigate the water without the aid of wind or tide; and so positive was he in his objections, and they were based on such absolute knowledge (want of knowledge), that he proposed to eat the first steamboat, captain, crew, and all hands, that crossed the Atlantic. Men, however, nothing daunted at the threat of this old musty fogy, launched their boats; and, even to this day, steamboats float on British waters.

When the magnetic telegraph was first talked of, there were thousands of persons in this country who could prove the thing impossible. Long lists of objections were presented; "the letters could not get around or through the posts." Even if this objection could be removed, there were hundreds of others quite as formidable. The telegraph, even including the Atlantic cable, has gone into successful operation; and now there is hardly a man in the world who did not always know it could be done.

Thirty years ago, there were thousands of church people who could prove that slavery was a "divine institution," and abolitionism an insane, infidel, dangerous heresy, originating under the direct influence of his Satanic Majesty, and leading the people by thousands to the bottomless pit. We should now expect objectors to know as much of Spiritualism.

To a few of the most popular and strong objections, we will now pay our respects.

Objection No. 1. — God anciently made laws against getting knowledge from the dead.

The precepts to which objectors refer may be found in the following words: —

"When thou art come into the land which the Lord thy God giveth thee, thou shalt not learn to do after the abominations of those nations. There shall not be found among you any one that maketh his son or his daughter to pass through the fire, or that useth divination, or an observer of times, or an enchanter, or a witch, *or a charmer, or a consulter with familiar spirits, or a wizard, or a necromancer.* For all that do these things are an abomination unto the Lord; and because of these abominations the Lord thy God doth drive them out from before thee." — Deut. xviii. 9–12.

"Regard not them that have familiar spirits, neither seek after wizards, to be defiled by them: I am the Lord your God." — Lev. xix. 31.

"And the soul that turneth after such as have familiar spirits, and after wizards, to go a whoring after them, I will even set my face against that soul, and will cut him off from among his people." — Lev. xx. 6.

"And when they shall say unto you, Seek unto them that have familiar spirits, and unto wizards that peep and that mutter: should not a people seek unto their God? for the living to the dead? To the law and to the testimony: if they speak not according to this word, it is because there is no light in them." — Isa. viii. 19, 20.

We have quoted all these paragraphs in order to give the reader the full force of the objection; for, if we can read our own heart, we have no design to keep back a word or thought that could in any way assist the objector. These Scriptures can not easily be misunderstood. The first paragraph emphatically forbids necromancy, or the consulting of familiar spirits. Necromancy comes from two Greek words, *nekros*, which means "dead," and *mantia*, the definition of which is "divination." Divination, Webster defines as follows: "the act of divining, a foretelling of future events, the discovering things secret or obscure by the aid of superior beings or by other than human means."

It will be seen by these definitions, that the Mosaic law forbade those under its jurisdiction getting knowledge from the dead.

God is, or is not, the author of this law: if he is not its author, it should no more be quoted as authority here than though it occurred in the Mohammedan Koran. The laws against Salem witchcraft have as much authority in the investigation of Spiritualism as this, unless God is directly or indirectly its author. But, if God is its author, it follows that he made laws against obtaining knowledge from the dead. Now, God certainly will not be accused of legislating against an *ignis fatuus*. If, as some suppose, the dead are totally unconscious, there would be no danger of people holding converse with them; hence no necessity for this law. If, on the other hand, the dead are conscious, but can not hold intercourse with the living, there would be no necessity for this law. Whether the law is opposed to modern Spiritualism will be seen as we proceed. Two things are positively settled by this law.

First, the Hebrews were inclined to apply to the dead for knowledge; else there would have been no necessity for this enactment. Paul says, "The law is made for the disobedient" (1 Tim. i. 9). This is positive proof that they knew the *fact* of spirit-intercourse, and some of them believed in its utility, insomuch that it was necessary to have such a law.

Second, the power making this law received the fact, or, instead of this law accompanied with these reasons, he would have informed them of their mistake.

Wherever this law originated, it was a part of the law which was only "added because of transgression, until the seed should come" (Gal. iii. 19). This law has been found unworthy of a place in the divine economy, and is among the things which have been abolished. (Eph. ii. 15; Col. ii. 14.) Is it possible that our Christian friends are going to arraign and condemn Spiritualists for violating an old dead Jewish law? If Spiritualists are guilty of a great crime in violating that law, what shall be done with Christians? for the law is not any more positive in forbidding Spiritualism than in its prohibition of working on Saturday; of mixing linen and wool together in garments; of eating of swine's flesh and catfish. (Ex. xx. 10; Lev. xi. 7–11.) This same law emphatically forbids a man to mar as much as the corners of his beard; but many Christians, and even ministers, who oppose Spiritualism because of precepts in the same law, shave two or three times every week of their lives. See Lev. xix. 27.

If the law forbidding spirit-communion was divine, and of lasting obligation, then Jesus broke a divine law; for he did hold a *tête-à-tête* with Moses and Elias after they had each been in the spirit-world several centuries. Paul also violated, when he conversed with Jesus after he had spent several years in the higher life; and John, for holding a conversation with his brother, deserved a punishment no less than death. (Lev. xx. 6.) Will the objector, for the sake of carrying out his objection, accuse all the New-Testament saints of violating the law of God?

Now, we believe there are reasons (some of them good, and some not so good) for giving this law. If the objector should hear a father say to his eight-year-old child, "You shall not study algebra," would he, from that, conclude that the father was opposed to the study of algebra, or only that the child was not yet developed up to that study; that minor studies must be conquered first? And what would you think of the child, who, ten years after the father had said he should not study algebra, upon being requested by his teacher to enter upon the higher branches of mathematics, should respond, "It's wicked; my father forbade it long ago"?

The case in our illustration is similar to the one produced by the objector. The race was younger then than now, and was not educated up to the point where unlimited spirit-communication would not, with its good, have a mixture of evil. Men in those days believed that every spirit who communicated was a god; indeed, this was the way Jehovah, the Jewish God, got his infinity. We can not see how any one can read the description of the person and character of this God, who presided over the Hebrew nation, without coming to the conclusion that he was either a myth or a departed human spirit. It is to be doubted whether the Jews would not have been a better people, had they not had such implicit confidence in their Jehovah. It was their

God who said to Moses, "Avenge the children of Israel of the Midianites: afterward shalt thou be gathered unto thy people." — Num. xxxi. 2.

This God goes on giving commands, which were fulfilled as follows: —

"And they warred against the Midianites, as the Lord commanded Moses; and they slew all the males. And they slew the kings of Midian, beside the rest of them that were slain; namely, Evi and Rekem and Zur and Hur and Reba, five kings of Midian: Balaam, also, the son of Beor, they slew with the sword. And the children of Israel took all the women of Midian captives, and their little ones; and took the spoil of all their cattle, and all their flocks, and all their goods. And they burnt all their cities wherein they dwelt, and all their goodly castles, with fire." — Num. xxxi. 7–10.

Notwithstanding this wholesale butchery, and burning of cities, the Lord was in a rage because they had not been more heartless, and told Moses to say, —

"Now, therefore, kill every male among the little ones, and kill every woman that hath known man by lying with him. But all the women-children that have not known a man by lying with him, keep alive for yourselves." — Num. xxxi. 17, 18.

The reading of this Scripture shows that their implicit confidence in their God led them to commit deeds of darkness, which, left to themselves, they were not bloodthirsty enough to undertake. This is proof positive, not only that they were led to deeds of crime by their belief in the infallibility of communications coming from their Jehovah, but that that God could not have been the Author of the universe. Undoubtedly, a leading reason why the prohibition against seeking the dead for knowledge was given could be found in the following language: —

"For thou shalt worship no other god; for the Lord, whose name is Jealous, is a jealous God. Lest thou make a covenant with the inhabitants of the land, and they go a whoring after their gods, and do sacrifice unto their gods, and one call thee, and thou eat of his sacrifice; and thou take of their daughters unto thy sons, and their daughters go a whoring after their gods, and make thy sons go a whoring after their gods." — Ex. xxxiv. 14–16.

Here the gods of the land are recognized as being gods in every sense that this jealous-hearted Jewish God can claim that title. The God of whom it is said, "And the Lord came down to see the city and the tower which the children of men builded" (Gen. xi. 6), is not the Author of the universe. The following language is a better description of a bigoted, jealous human spirit than of the Creator of heaven and earth: —

"And the Lord said unto Moses, Go, get thee down; for thy people, which thou broughtest out of the land of Egypt, have corrupted themselves; they have turned aside quickly out of the way which I commanded them; they have made them a molten calf, and have worshiped it, and have sacrificed thereunto, and said, These be thy gods, O Israel, which have brought thee up out of the land of Egypt. And the Lord said unto Moses, I have seen this people, and, behold, it is a stiffnecked people: now, therefore, let me alone, that my wrath may wax hot against them, and that I may consume them; and I will make of thee a great nation. And Moses besought the Lord his God, and said, Lord, why doth thy wrath wax hot against thy people, which thou hast brought forth out of the land of Egypt with great power, and with a mighty hand? Wherefore should the Egyptians speak, and say, For mischief did he bring them out; to slay them in the mountains, and to consume them from the face of the earth? Turn from thy fierce wrath, and repent of this evil against thy people. Remember Abraham, Isaac, and Israel, thy servants, to whom thou swarest by thine own self, and saidst unto them, I will multiply your seed as the stars of heaven, and all this land that I have spoken of I will give unto your seed, and they shall inherit it for ever. And the Lord repented of the evil which he thought to do unto his people." — Ex. xxxii. 7–14.

No one now worships a God who was so spiteful and changeable as this representation of the Deity. Moses, in this instance, is decidedly the superior in every sense of the word. God acknowledges it, by yielding to Moses' superior wisdom, and not doing what *he thought* he would do unto his people. We do not say this ignorant bigot, calling himself God, was not Jehovah: that, for aught we know, might have been his name; but we do say that this whiffling, jealous Deity has not sense enough to govern the world. This is abundantly proved by his changing his plan of action in obedience to the superior wisdom of Moses.

The heathen gods were once men upon earth. After passing to the world of spirits, and returning and manifesting themselves, they were at once recognized as deities, and, of course, esteemed infallible. Spiritualism, to-day, would do more harm than good if every

Spiritualist received as infallible every communication coming from that source: hence, until people arrive at the position where they can take the spirits as *helps*, *teachers*, not *masters*, they are not prepared for communion with them. Let authority give place to *reason*, and men weigh communications from the other shore as they do advice from friends here, and communications from spirits can do no more harm than would result from friend counseling with friend in this life.

The Jews, quite as much as any other nation, were inclined to worship every spirit that communicated. Abraham and Lot each bowed to the earth before the angels which came to them. When an angel, who was emphatically called a man, appeared to Joshua, the record says, —

"And Joshua fell on his face to the earth, and did worship, and said unto him, What saith my lord unto his servant?" — Josh. v. 14.

When Peter saw Moses and Elias on the mount, his first exclamation was, —

"Lord, it is good for us to be here: if thou wilt, let us make here three tabernacles; one for thee, and one for Moses, and one for Elias." — Matt. xvii. 4.

As much as to say, "When we would worship you, we would go into one of these tabernacles; when we would worship Moses, we would go into another; and, when we would worship Elias, we would go into another." When John saw his brother a prophet, he fell at his feet to worship him. With that idea, the Spiritualism of to-day would lead to idolatry, and hence be wrong; but Spiritualists have advanced to where they can treat their spirit-friends as familiar friends, and yet not receive them as authority. With this advancement, we claim that spirit-communion can not result in harm: those who have not got so far along would do well to let it alone.

The law forbidding spirit-communion had its evil as well as its good results. While it may have kept the Jews from idolatry, and some other crimes that they otherwise might have committed, it drove many of their best minds into the most gross materialism. Had they been permitted to consult the dead, their best writers never could have said,—

"For the living know that they shall die: but the dead know not any thing, neither have they any more a reward; for the memory of them is forgotten. Also their love, and their hatred, and their envy, is now perished; neither have they any more a portion for ever in any thing that is done under the sun."—Eccl. ix. 5, 6.

Solomon was not the only writer who occasionally gave utterance to such infidel sentiments. Job and David more than once utter the same; but Elihu, both a clairvoyant and clairaudient medium, says,—

"Now a thing was secretly brought to me, and mine ear received a little thereof. In thoughts from the visions of the night, when deep sleep falleth on men, fear came upon me, and trembling, which made all my bones to shake. Then a spirit passed before my face; the hair of my flesh stood up: it stood still, but I could not discern the form thereof: an image was before mine eyes, there was silence, and I heard a voice, saying, Shall mortal man be more just than God? shall a man be more pure than his Maker? Behold, he put no trust in his servants; and his angels he charged with folly: how much less in them that dwell in houses of clay, whose foundation is in the dust, which are crushed before the moth?"—Job iv. 12–19.

This "spirit which passed before his face," causing him to quake and tremble, as hundreds of mediums now do, taught him the important lesson that men are not clay, but "dwell in houses of clay." Thus all can see the result, on the one hand, of spirit-communion, and, on the other, of its prohibition. All the texts usually produced by materialists to prove the dead unconscious are the result of the enactment against Spiritualism, and consequent non-intercourse with the dead.

Objection No. 2.—The Bible says,—

"Thus saith the Lord, Stand ye in the ways, and see, and ask for the old paths, where is the good way, and walk therein, and ye shall find rest for your souls."—Jer. vi. 16.

It does not do to forsake the "old paths." Spiritualism is new; if true, it should have been discovered prior to the nineteenth century.

It sounds a little strange to hear this objection urged by the same speaker, and almost in the same breath with the one just noticed. Many of the opponents of Spiritualism seem to have lost their regard for consistency, if not for truth. In one breath, Spiritualism is an old sin God was compelled more than three thousand years ago to put down by legislation; in the next it is something new, and for that reason they have gone to work with such zeal to tear it to pieces that one would almost think they would pluck a new moon from the heavens if it were in their power to do so. Consistency is too rare a jewel to come into general use among those who have enlisted in the battle against the angel-world. If Spiritualism is an invention of the nineteenth century, the last delusion of the Devil, God did not make laws against it in the days of Moses. On the other hand, if laws were made against it then, the objection of "new things" is *ad captandum.*

Has the objector ever considered that there are swords that have two edges? that, when persons go it blind, they occasionally catch an argument by the blade, and cut their own fingers? Such is the fact in this case.

Suppose Spiritualism to be a child of the nineteenth century: the argument of new things weighed as heavily against Jesus and his associates as it now does against Spiritualism. Christianity was so new in the days of Paul, that it is said of certain philosophers, —

"And they took him, and brought him unto Areopagus, saying, May we know what this new doctrine whereof thou speakest is? For thou bringest certain strange things to our ears: we would know, therefore, what these things mean. For all the Athenians, and strangers which were there, spent their time in nothing else, but either to tell or to hear some new thing." — Acts xvii. 19–21.

Every thing had a beginning, and was new in the days of its infancy. We remember to have heard a learned professor say, "Monkeys existed before men, and fishes are older than philosophers." Protestantism in the days of Martin Luther was new, and Catholicism was old: what Protestant thence concludes his own religion false, and Catholicism true?

Had the "old path" argument used by our Catholic

fathers had the desired effect, there would not have been a Protestant in the world to-day. Ministers who are now preaching against Spiritualism because of its novelty, would, in that case, have been confessing their sins to a Catholic priest, and we to-day would have been eating the actual body and drinking the blood of Jesus Christ, and enduring a tyranny such as is only known within the limits of the "Eternal City."

When Martin Luther first made his discoveries, Lutheranism was new, and, per consequence, every follower of Martin Luther was either a knave, fool, or fanatic, as could be proved by every Catholic priest in the Old World. Lutheranism, however, spread, notwithstanding the barking of Catholic dogs. A century was quite sufficient to kill the cry of "Novelty;" and Protestantism could be respected and venerated because of its age. Lutheranism is not alone; other religious theories must run the same gantlet. When Methodism first began to force itself upon the people, it, too, was a new invention of the Devil to lead fanatics to hell: this could be proved by every Roman Catholic, Presbyterian, or Baptist in the land. Methodism has lived a century; and, as a result, those who abominated it, and would have sent every "fanatical Methodist" to hell (but words could not do it), now respect it as "our sister church."

If all the theories in the world have lived through the warfare against new things, we will risk but that Spiritualism will take deeper root and grow more healthy and beautiful as a result of this attack.

Now, admitting that Spiritualism is new, is its novelty against its truth? We think not. Men existed on the earth *at least one hundred and fifty thousand years* before they learned to communicate with each other by means of the electric telegraph; yet who refused to receive the news of Lee's surrender, because, a century since, it would have taken it a month to go from Richmond to Chicago? Persons will accept of improvements everywhere except in religious matters: how strange! Are all who have died fools? Supposing they could not have communicated prior to 1848: men in this world have made many discoveries since that time; may not those on the other side have discovered something? Mesmer, who discovered the science of mesmerism, and Benjamin Franklin, who taught men how to control the lightning, are each in the land of the so-called dead. Now, while Prof. Morse was discovering and perfecting a new mode of communication between mortals, why can not Newton, Franklin, and others discover a plan by which the dead and living can converse? Certainly such a discovery would be of vast importance; then why object?

But Spiritualism is not new: it is traced through all time, and found among all people. We have not the space here to devote to this proposition. The reader who is curious to look into this department of the subject is requested to go or send to the bookstore of Colby & Rich, No. 9 Montgomery Place, Boston, and get some of their numerous books on this question.

It is enough for us here to say that phenomenal Spiritualism was patent in the days of Luther. Who has not read the account of Luther seizing and throwing an inkstand at a spirit whom he supposed to be the Devil? The manifestations in the Wesley family, an account of which John Wesley himself records, were quite equal to those occurring in the family of John D. Fox. Dr. Adam Clarke, Carvosso, and other Methodist divines, record as wonderful spirit-manifestations as there are in the year 1869.

Objection No. 3. — These manifestations are from the Devil. Paul says, —

"Even him whose coming is after the working of Satan, with all power and signs and lying wonders." — 2 Thess. ii. 9.

John says, —

"They are spirits of devils, working miracles, which go forth unto the kings of the earth, and of the whole world, to the battle of the great day of God Almighty." — Rev. xvi. 14.

The charge of demoniac possession, like the "new things" argument, is an old one. When John the Baptist commenced his work, the popular church said, "He hath a devil" (Matt. xi. 18). When Jesus came, speaking as never man spake, and doing as never man did, a hypocritical church said, "This fellow doth not cast out devils but by Beelzebub the prince of the devils." — Matt. xii. 24.

Jesus gave his followers to understand that this ever would be the case. He said, "If they have called the master of the house Beelzebub, how much more shall they call them of his household?" — Matt. x. 25.

With this warning in advance, and a knowledge that our predecessors in every work of reform have endured the same charge, we are bold to endure such charges. If the Church of all ages can be believed, the Devil has originated and put into successful operation every reform, and that in spite of the Church, which has ever been faithful to warn its dupes that every reformer was the especial agent of his Satanic Majesty.

According to the church of Jesus' time he had a devil: but he and his devil succeeded in putting his work into successful operation, and matters went on swimmingly, until they succeeded in calling out a large party of followers; but, in proportion as they increased in numbers and power, they became corrupt, until the so-called Christian Church became so terribly wicked, that the Devil would have nothing further to do with it. His Majesty left them to "paddle their own canoe," and began anon to work through heretics, who were compelled, on account of their good works, to leave the Church.

During the whole period known as the dark ages, there was not a martyr burned at the stake, but that was under the influence of the Devil. That word "devil" has always served as a scapegoat to pack its ignorance and hatred of progress on. It requires no tact or learning to say "devil," and it often does to explain various phenomena hidden behind that word. This is, perhaps, the main reason why the old gentleman has had so much to carry. Even Martin Luther told his followers that the Copernican system of astronomy, including the rotundity of the earth, was directly from the Devil.

The telescope was of satanic origin. The first fanning-mill was "a wicked invention to raise the Devil's wind." The inventor was informed, that, if he wanted to separate his wheat and chaff, he should get down upon his knees, and ask God to send him a good dispensation of air; or, if not humble enough to do that, to patiently wait until God in his mercy chose to send him wind. Notwithstanding the windmill was the Devil's invention, it soon gained such a hold on the populace, that a Presbyterian could, without any scruples of conscience, eat bread made of the wheat which had passed through the Devil's windmill. We would not be understood as representing that the Church sanctioned or even *tolerated* such impiety. It did not. Ever faithful to its duty, the Church disfellowshiped every member who had so far followed his diabolical leadership as to eat the bread made of wheat which had been cleansed by this "infernal machine." Alas for the weakness of man! how soon is he led astray! The Devil's windmill has become so popular, that ministers use bread, even in the communion service, that was made of the wheat which had gone through the Devil's windmill. Thus the Devil always carries the day.

The man who first applied water to the propelling of a sawmill was put to death for being in league with the Devil. The first printing-press was invented and run by tho Devil. It was the Devil, who, through Harvey, discovered the circulation of the blood. This same Devil enabled Michael Servetus to discover that a mathematical impossibility could not be a theological truth. When this agent of his Majesty the Devil was told that in the Godhead there were three persons at *least*, and only one at *most*, he was inclined to doubt it, and wondered if that would not lead to the idea of *three Gods.* "Oh, no!" the response was: "there is but one God, and he is made of three distinct individualities." — "Well, taking either of these three separately, would he be a God, an angel, or a man?" His questions were too well put: none but a Devil could invent such questions. When he was asked to sing, —

"Have faith the same,
With endless shame,
For all the human race;
For hell is crammed
With infants damned,
Without a day of grace,"

he dared to question the truth of the song, and the propriety of singing it. He was at once set down for a Devil-possessed heretic, and condemned to death. John Calvin, after signing his death-warrant, led the mob that burned him over a slow fire, for the crime of disputing old theories. As usual, the Devil in this was successful. The whole world now acknowledge that Servetus was right, and Calvin and his horde of bigoted followers wrong.

"The world goes round and round,
The genial seasons run,
And ever the truth comes uppermost,
And ever is justice done."

It was in the present century that ministers came out in long printed statements (for by this time the Devil had made his printing-press popular enough for their use) to prove that vaccination to prevent small-pox was an invention of the Devil to change men to a kind of quadruped; that vaccination would surely result in producing horns on the heads of those who submitted to any such satanic operation to prevent this dreaded contagion. The Devil originated the science of geology, set on foot the abolition movement; in fact, has led every band of reformers in the world. Now, his last great work is in Spiritualism. All we have to say is, Let him work. He has ever proved himself right, and we have confidence to believe it ever will be thus; that is, if he has figured as largely in every new movement as he has been accused of doing.

Now, admitting for the sake of the argument, the existence, power, and malignity of this almighty Devil, how is the fact to be harmonized with the existence, power, wisdom, and goodness of our loving Father? Whatever may be said of Spiritualists now, millions of them were once honest and earnest praying Christians. For years and years, they made it their daily duty to turn to their God and Bible: they have read again and again, —

"And I say unto you, Ask, and it shall be given you; seek, and ye shall find; knock, and it shall be opened unto you. For every one that asketh, receiveth; and he that seeketh, findeth; and to him that knocketh it shall be opened. If a son shall ask bread of any of you that is a father, will he give him a stone? or, if he ask a fish, will he for a fish give him a serpent? or, if he shall ask an egg, will he offer him a scorpion? If ye then, being evil, know how to give good gifts unto your children; how much more shall your heavenly Father give the Holy Spirit to them that ask him?" — Luke xi. 9–13.

Is this the way the All-Father has answered their prayers after telling them that if they would ask they should receive? They have prayed earnestly for the Holy Ghost, have ever been willing to take this prayer-hearing God at his word; and God has answered their prayer by opening the *infernal regions*, and peopling the air with *quintillions* of devils, whose only object is to deceive and lead the elect to hell, our angel-friends meantime being shut up in heaven, away from earth, weeping to see us deluded by deceiving spirits, and that in answer to our most sincere and devout prayers a thousand times repeated. Is this the God our opposers worship? Is faith such a heartless cheat, baring the back thus for the Devil's rod? In Heaven's name, if God is such a knave as this idea represents, it is well to serve the Devil! We would not worship such a God if we could, and certainly could not if we would. That father who hands out myriads of scorpions and vipers to his weeping, starving children, is an angel of light compared with this treacherous knave called God, who thus deceives his trusting children.

Nay, we will go farther, and apply this argument even to the existence of his Satanic Majesty. If the Devil exists, he exists either by the will and power of God or contrary to it. If he exists by the power of God, then God is responsible for all of his actions: he permits him to act when he could prevent it. We consider ourself responsible for all the evil there is in the world which we could prevent: so of God. But if Satan is *eternal* and *almighty*, if he exists contrary to the will of God, then God lacks either the power or wisdom to prevent the Devil deceiving and leading the world to hell. In one case, God is wicked; in the other, weak.

If the Church has been wrong in its cry of "Devil!" after every reform, it may be in this. If, on the other hand, it was right, then we are proud of our leader: he has proved himself right in every instance, and we will trust him in this. Progress is the order of the day; and one only needs to read his history to be convinced that he is not only a progressionist, but the author of progress. Commencing with his first work, which was to open the eyes of a pair of poor blind idiots in the garden of Eden, and teach them to know good from evil, and ending the drama with Spiritualism, we indorse every act of his. We are proud to-day to take our position beside "Michael the archangel," and not bring a "railing accusation against him." May he long live to put in motion all the latent machinery of human progress!

Reader, we can not close this chapter without saying, in all candor, your Devil is only a myth. Give the frontal brain the control of the back brain, and all the devils and satyrs will flee. They can not stand before well-developed causality and comparison.

That reader and writer may be enabled to resist all the devils growing out of a "lack of knowledge;" that we may be enabled to see the hand of God in the wide field of human progress, and co-operate with the powers beyond in leading the people out of the devilish bondage of ignorance and superstition, we most earnestly pray.

www.ingramcontent.com/pod-product-compliance
Lightning Source LLC
LaVergne TN
LVHW050520100826
845148LV00002B/399

* 9 7 8 1 4 2 5 5 2 0 7 5 5 *